TABLE OF CONTENTS

LIST OF FIGURES

LIST OF TABLES

I. INTRODUCTION

A. INTRODUCTION TO THE PROBLEM

The sudden increase in crime and violence in some Mexican cities and regions has raised security concerns not only in Mexico, where President Felipe Calderon categorized these crimes as a threat to Mexican society (Presidencia de la Republica Mexicana, 2007b), but also in the United States, where Department of Homeland Secretary head Janet Napolitano referred to stemming the violence as "vital to core U.S. national interests" (Napolitano & Department of Homeland Security, 2009). Mexico is concerned with the latent threat of violence spreading all over the nation, while the U.S. is trying to guard against spillover. Both governments are concerned by the increased violence and its impact on communities along the U.S.–Mexican border.

Due to its geopolitically important location, Mexico has historically received fallout from undesired, second-degree effects of some U.S. strategies (Moreno, 2009; Smith, 2008). These unintended consequences are called "balloon effects" because they can be compared to the dynamics inside a balloon when a force applied to one spot sends air pressure to a weaker place inside the balloon (Kenneth, 2010; Whitworth, 2008).

Paradoxically, when the Mexican government developed its strategy to confront transnational organized crime in 2006, this path changed notably, sending the pressure of the balloon effect in two directions; first, inside Mexico, where the strategy unbalanced the criminal structure, creating balloon effects inside Mexican territory, and second, sending the pressure of the balloon effect back to the U.S. while asking to escalate the Mexican government's effort, asking for help in improving its strategy to confront transnational organized crime (Brownfield, 2011c; United States Government Accountability Office, 2010).

This thesis will conduct a longitudinal case study of three U.S. strategies to demonstrate the reality of the balloon effect and describe its behavior and implications for Mexican homeland security, following the methodology presented by George and Bennett in their book, *Case Studies and Theory Development in the Social Science*

1

(2005). This thesis includes a single-case study of the 2007 Mexican strategy against transnational organized crime and its balloon-effect implications for Mexican homeland security, as well as the counter-pressure of the balloon effect inside the U.S.

According to the International Monetary Fund, the Americas contain two of the most advanced economies of the world; they also contain the Latin American countries, which are "emerging and/or developing economies" (International Monetary Fund, 2011). Consequently, Mexico's geopolitical location, as the southernmost country of North America and northernmost country of Latin America, makes it the least developed country in North America, but also the country with the highest internal gross product in Latin America.

In other words, Mexico is the geographical link between the advanced economies of North America, commonly known as "developed economies," and Latin America's "developing, or third world countries"—creating what Mihaela Ulieru describes as the "interdependent security ecosystem" (Ulieru, 2008).

With regard to the interdependence of security ecosystems, Ulieru suggests that the threats (challenges) of the twenty-first century are different from those in the past. Mechanisms employed to manage interaction among complex organizations, such as the military, are necessary to achieving a common goal, taking into consideration that human and organizational factors not always addressed at the macro level (Ulieru, 2008). With Ulieru, we can say that an interdependent security ecosystem drives governments to evaluate their options for confronting regional threats according to the capacity of each actor involved—which, in the case of America's security chain, has not always been duly considered.

In other words, we can say that Mexico's geopolitical location gives her a proximity disadvantage in terms of the Pan-American, interdependent, security ecosystem, turning it the weakest link in the security chain.

This thesis also includes a single-case study of the 2007 Mexican strategy against transnational organized crime and its balloon-effect implications for Mexican homeland security, as well as the counter-pressure of the balloon effect inside the U.S.

Following the same strategy the U.S. has been using for more than 40 years in its war on drugs, the Mexican government confronted the drug problem at production sites and transportation routes, creating balloon effects at the meso and micro levels inside Mexico, as well as at the macro level in the international arena.

B.   THE BALLOON EFFECT

In the security field, the concept of the balloon effect refers to the second order effects, "A," caused by the behavior of a threat "B," that due to the pressure applied, "C," at its original location, "D." has to migrate to a different location "E," trying to perform the same activities, "F," at a new destination, "G."

Specifically, the concept of the balloon effect refers to desired and undesired second-order effects (A) such as the increment of violence on the streets, caused by the behavior of an agent (B), such as a fight among cartel members. Due to pressure (C), such as high-impact operations against transnational organized crime at areas of influence in a given location (D), criminals must migrate to a different location (E), such as the Mexican–U.S. border, in an effort to continue their activities (F), at a new destination (G).

Balloon effects are not related to the normal migration patterns of urban or economic redistribution; this concept, according to Dennis Epple and Glenn J. Platt, is focused on the equilibrium and redistribution in a local system where households differ by both preferences and income (Epple & Platt, 1998).

Instances of balloon effects, as described in this research, are: the 1882 U.S. Chinese-Exclusion Act, which sent thousands of Chinese to Mexico (Pardo, 2008); Operation Intercept of 1969, against American marijuana consumption, which not only provoked chaos over the main crossing points along the Mexican–U.S. border, but also in local, national, and international politics (Toro, 1992); and the North America Free-Trade Agreement (NAFTA) of 1994, which put Mexico on an equal basis with the U.S. and Canadian economy, creating an openness paradox—the dilemma of remaining open while maintaining security and bringing, not only economic activity, but security problems into the country (Bayle, 2005).

C.   THE BALLOON EFFECT IN THE SECURITY FIELD

In the cases mentioned, the balloon effect in the security field has been strongly experienced between Mexico and the U.S., specifically at the border region. It has also been mentioned in many U.S. government documents (Interdepartmental Task Force, 1969; Napolitano & Department of Homeland Security, 2009; U.S. Department of Justice, National Intelligence Center, 2011; U.S. State Department, 2009) and used by authors, such as Gabriela Toro and Peter Smith, to explain migratory and secondary or collateral effects that are caused by an agent in one location and experienced as pressure in another. However, neither of these authors created a specific definition of this useful and explicit idea.

The ambiguous presentation of the balloon effect caused authors Whitworth and Michel to include a partial interpretation of the concept in their thesis (Kenneth, 2010; Whitworth, 2008). Whitworth described the balloon effect as the movement of drug trafficking to a new venue, or the shifting power between drug organizations as a consequence of "tactical successes and strategic failures." Kenneth used the term to explain why "U.S. antidrug policies are unlikely to reduce the amount of drugs that enter the U.S. market over the long term" and the "huge impact on the distribution of profits from the drug trade" (Kenneth, 2010; Whitworth, 2008). Both argued that, following the balloon effect, problem and the profits would migrate; yet both confined themselves to the causes of the balloon effect, that is, the secondary effects as pressure in one region migrates to another.

In this thesis, we deal with the second part of the balloon effect. The recipient country or region creates counter-pressure in trying to confront the balloon effects on its own soil. This counter-pressure, a natural response to the flow from a stronger to a weaker point, commonly stems from U.S. strategies whose fallout has flowed elsewhere (Foot, MacFarlane, & Mastanduno, 2003) and has been looked at strictly in those terms. In contrast, we here analyze the pressure applied to the U.S. government by the balloon effects of Mexican high-impact operations against transnational crime.

4

According to the President Calderon's 2011 address to the nation, the operation's success is forcing criminal organizations to fight among them as they compete for places to perform their activities (Presidencia de la Republica Mexicana, 2011). These fights are causing casualties not only to federal and police forces but among civilians (CNN, 2010). Increased violence in the streets of Mexico is considered a threat to the U.S., due to the risk of its crossing the border (Brownfield, 2011b).

Some illustrations of the balloon effect resulting from policies developed by the U.S. follow. An example of the counter-pressure of the 1882 Chinese immigration into Mexico might be the tunnels build by the Chinese to traffic illegal substances over the border during Prohibition (Cummings, 2001). Another example is the resurgence of the Mexican drug cartels in the early 2000s as a consequence of the Colombian plan (Correspondent, 2010; Fieser, 2010; Kenney, 2007). And , finally, the most recent case is the increased violence in Mexico since 2006, a consequence of the Mexican "high-impact operations" against transnational organized crime and the counter-pressure felt by the U.S. government. Citing the balloon-effect phenomenon, authors like Gabriela Moreno note that national and regional strategies against drugs may feed a vicious cycle in Latin America (Moreno, 2009; Smith, 2008; Toro, 1992), based mainly on the following observations:

- Drug consumption does not decrease.
- Drug use changes every time a new strategy is developed against some specific type of drug.
- Prices are not greatly affected.
- Production sites and routes merely migrate.
- The business remains highly profitable.

Following the same line of reasoning, this thesis explores the balloon effect in relation to Mexican homeland security, beginning when current Mexican president Felipe Calderón Hinojoza came into power in December 2006 and changed Mexico's situation with regard to the Americas' security chain.

As part of its national-security strategy, President Calderón's administration developed high-impact operations against transnational, organized crime (Presidencia de la Republica Mexicana, 2007). These are joint operations at the national level, among the Mexican armed forces: navy, army, and police; and at three levels of government: federal, state, and local. Those operations represent one part of the holistic approach taken by the Mexican government against criminal organizations that challenge not only the government of Mexico, but all governments where they perform their activities and threaten society.

As a further implication of this strategic decision at the national level, President Calderon's administration upgraded the effort by asking for U.S. assistance (Presidencia de la Republica Mexicana, 2011; U.S. State Department, 2009). Consequently, in 2007, the governments of Mexico, the U.S., and the nations of Central America, the Dominican Republic, and Haiti developed the Merida Initiative (Ribando Seelke & Finklea, 2011; United States Government Accountability Office, 2010). This action can be considered a counter-flow of the balloon effect, this time instigated by the Mexican government, using the same approach the U.S. has been taking for more than 40 years since 1969s Operation Intercept. According to Richard Craig, Operation Intercept was created to battle drugs in production and in-route countries (Craig, 1980), the same approach used in Mexican high-impact operations.

D.   THE BALLOON-EFFECT BEGINNING

Since the establishment of the Monroe Doctrine in 1823, the U.S. has been trying to refine a Western-Hemispheric hegemony policy through the use of political, economic, and sometimes military support to countries in Latin America (Foot, MacFarlane, & Mastanduno, 2003; Griffith, 1997; Malone & Khong, 2001) This doctrine is perceived as a type of friendly coercion, and the U.S. has used its supremacy as a weapon to enhance what Joseph Nye Jr. (2004) calls "soft power" over Latin America.

Nye states in his book, *Bound to Lead: The Changing Nature of American Power*, that the U.S. is not only the strongest nation in military and economic terms, but also in terms of its ability to achieve its goals through attractive means rather than coercion (2004). Nye calls soft power "the ability to influence the behavior of others to accomplish the outcomes one wants." In this sense, Nye states that soft power "could be developed through relations with allies, economic assistance, and cultural exchanges" (2004). Under the Monroe Doctrine of "America for the Americans," and using Nye's definition of "soft power," every time the U.S. develops a strategy, whether unilaterally or in conjunction with other nations, some balloon effects are felt in Mexican territory, provoking what Peter Smith calls "complex questions of historical causalities" (Smith, 2008).

By looking at the situation from a broad spectrum, we can find that the Western Hemisphere has been influenced by dominant U.S. power. The Monroe Doctrine established the foundation of subsequent strategies, to the point where, embedded in the 2011 U.S. National Security Strategy, we still find traces of this doctrine, due to American technological advances, military power, social and political stability, and economic influence. Soft power (Nye, 2004) reflects an existing gap, particularly between the U.S. and the less-developed countries of Latin America, giving the U.S. a very comfortable "geopolitical stability in [the] Americas" (P. H. Smith, 2008).

U.S. action against illegal substances can be traced back to 1867, when the general court of Massachusetts created one of the oldest acts against alcohol, added to the Constitution as the Eighteenth Amendment in 1919. Since then, many strategies have been developed by the U.S., alone or in cooperation with other countries, to control alcohol and drug problems.

It was in 1823, however—almost 200 years ago—that, under the Monroe Doctrine, the U.S. tried to use its dominant position to impose its point of view over the rest of the Americas. This was confirmed in 1969, when President Nixon implemented Operation Intercept, focusing on production and transportation of illicit drugs (Nixon, 1969). But even when U.S. strategies against the drug business enjoy success, none have reached the goal of decreasing drug consumption in the U.S., particularly among youth (Office of National Drug Control Policy, 2011).

Thus, while the U.S. approach is ineffective in breaking the chain of drug supply versus consumption (U.S. Department of Justice, National Intelligence Center, 2011), the lack of a holistic approach to the problem has created negative balloon effects in Mexican homeland security, reinforcing the hypothesis that Mexico is the weak link in the security chain of the Americas (Fowler, 1996; Smith, 2008).

E.   THE BALLOON-EFFECT COUNTER-PRESSURE

The Merida Initiative represents a paradoxical point in the fight against transnational organized crime because it was created at Mexican government request (Brownfield, 2011a; U.S. State Department, 2009). This action can be considered the first counter-flow of the balloon effect because it developed as a result of President Felipe Calderon's request for U.S. government assistance against activities threatening not only Mexico, but the region in general, by sending counter-pressure to the U.S. Based on this point of view, we can say that the Mexican strategy against transnational organized crime unbalanced the criminal structure, altering the vicious cycle (Anderson & Johnson, 1997). According to Anderson and Johnson, any system will remain balanced until some external intervention unbalances it, creating intended and unintended consequences and bringing not only positive, but negative, balloon effects, such as increased violence in some Mexican regions.

F.   BALLOON-EFFECT COMMON GROUND

Misinterpretation of the balloon effects and of the success of operations could be the reason behind Mexican society´s perception that the core causes of today's violence lie with Calderon's decision to use the Mexican armed forces against drug crime (Turbiville, 2007). According to a Mitofsky poll conducted in April 2010, 60 percent of Mexicans believe the rise of street violence represents a failed strategy against transnational organized crime (Campos, 2010). Jorge Carrasco and Reyes Garcés go a step further, tracing the casualties to "unattainable victory" (Carrasco, 2011; Reyes, 2009) and trying to diminish the effort of the Mexican government.

G.   METHODOLOGY

Following the methodology presented by George and Bennett in their book *Case Studies and Theory Development in the Social Science*s (George & Bennett, 2005), the main challenges of this thesis are:

- To test the hypothesis of whether the implications of the balloon effects resulting from U.S. strategies in the security field affected Mexican homeland security, making it the weakest link in the Americas' security chain;

- To test whether the new concept of balloon-effect counter-pressure coming from the Mexican strategy is influencing latent balloon effects against U.S. homeland security;

- To test whether those balloon effects created by the Mexican strategy inside Mexico are a positive measure of effectiveness for the strategy in the short term and a positive indicator of long-term victory.

From the analytical point of view established by George and Bennett, this thesis will define the set of variables and conditions to develop a three-case longitudinal study to explore whether the balloon effects of U.S. strategies had implications at the macro level in the Mexican homeland. Following the same logic, we will develop a single-case study to analyze whether increased violence on the streets is a balloon effect coming from Mexican strategy. If this is the case, what are the implications at the meso and micro levels of analysis, with regard to increased violence on the streets in some Mexican regions and cities? In an extended effort, we will analyze whether the balloon-effect counter-pressure from Mexican strategy has influenced the implementation of the Merida Initiative at the macro level of analysis.

Finally, we will try to determine if the fight among the cartels, leaders captured and/or extradited, cartels dismantled, and drugs, money, and guns interdicted are positive measures of effectiveness and measures of performance and can lead us to expect a long-term victory against transnational organized crime.

H.   PRELIMINARY ASSUMPTIONS

- The U.S. has used its hemispheric hegemony policy to develop strategies against what it sees as a threat without considering the balloon effects reaching other countries or regions in Latin America.

- Mexico has been the recipient of balloon effects, and therefore Mexico, due to its geopolitical location, can be considered the weakest link in the Americas' security chain.

- The Merida Initiative is a balloon effect's counter-pressure strategy that considers the positive and negative aspects of previous strategies and it can be considered a lessons-learned strategy.

9

- The increased violence in the streets of some Mexican regions and cities is a sufficient factor to be considered a balloon effect coming from the Mexican strategy against transnational organized crime, but an unnecessary reason to consider it a failed strategy.

I.   EXPECTED FINDINGS

- Mexico has been influenced by balloon effects stemming from different strategies.

- Mexican high-impact operations against transnational organized crime is a lesson-learned strategy from the macro level of analysis applied in Mexico with balloon effects at the meso and micro level and balloon-effect counter-pressure at the macro level of analysis inside the U.S.

J.   METHODOLOGICAL FOUNDATION

A longitudinal case study will focus on Mexico and the U.S., based on the close relationship and shared interest between the two countries (Smith, 2000). They were also chosen because, due to their different capacities, every time the U.S. seeks to develop a strategy to defend its security interests, Mexico has to identify its own options and alternatives while awaiting balloon effects, and later confront the threat migration in its own territory (P. H. Smith, 2008).

Mexico has its own case study because the current situation with regard to increased violence was a necessary and sufficient condition for the Mexican government to develop a strategy to confront transnational organized crime, creating balloon effects inside Mexico and balloon-effect counter-pressure inside the U.S. In terms of violence, those balloon effects have caused concerns about governability and border crossing. Consequently, the entire situation must be analyzed.

K.   OUTLINE

In order to present a coherent argument and understand Mexico's current situation, this thesis presents a methodology and framework to develop further arguments and ideas in Chapter II. Chapter III presents a longitudinal, deductive, case study of three cases: the 1882 U.S. Chinese-Exclusion Act, the 1969 U.S. Operation Intercept/Operation Cooperation, and the 1994 North American Free-Trade Agreement. In Chapter IV, we analyze Mexican security, considering a single-case study that represents a paradoxical point in time with respect to the international approach in the war of drugs. This case study will include Mexican high-impact operations and the upgraded Merida Initiative against transnational organized crime.

THIS PAGE INTENTIONALLY LEFT BLANK

II. FRAMEWORK AND METHODOLOGY

A. INTRODUCTION

In 1823, President James Monroe (1817–1825) created U.S. hegemony over the Western Hemisphere. According to analysts such as Gabriela Moreno, Maria Celia Toro, and Peter Smith, every time the U.S. applies its political, economic, or military influence in the Americas, other regions receive the impact in the form of "balloon effects" (Moreno, 2009; Smith, 2008; Toro, 1992).

Peter Smith, in *Talons of the Eagle: Latin America, the United States, and the World,* explains that these effects are based on the existing gap between the U.S. and Latin America (2008). Based on information presented by the International Monetary Fund, the U.S. is an "advanced economy" while the Latin American countries are "emerging and/or developing economies" (International Monetary Fund, 2011).

Apparently, based on historic cases, the balloon effects from some strategies have not been taken in consideration by decision makers during the planning process.

Based on the theory presented by Peter Schwartz in his book, *The Art Of The Long View* (1996), planning is an vital part of the strategic process because it helps to prevent what Mintzberg calls "future scenarios" and avoid what he considers "the entire beast" (Mintzberg, Ahlstrand, & Lampel, 1998).

According to the balloon-effect concept, the pressure exerted over any strategy's target will force it to move naturally when it feels the pressure or impact of the strategy. In other words, decision makers should consider that the target will not disappear, it will just move to a weaker point.

B. FRAMEWORK

Following a deductive theory-oriented research (George & Bennett, 2005), this thesis develops a three-case longitudinal study to analyze, at the international level, balloon effects on Mexican homeland security. Next, applying the same theory we analyze, in a separate, single-case study, the balloon effects caused by the Mexican government's strategy against transnational organized crime and its implications at the macro (international), meso (national), and micro (local) levels.

The longitudinal case study will help to demonstrate the balloon effect's implications when decision makers do not develop a holistic, long-view plan. This thesis will analyze the balloon effects resulting from some U.S. strategies, as well as the 2007 Mexican high-impact operations against transnational organized crime, trying to determine if they have affected the Mexican homeland and whether they have influenced counter balloon effect back in to U.S.

The final goal of this thesis is to explain the current Mexican situation with regard to the resurgence of transnational organized crime and the sudden increase of violence on the streets in some regions and cities.

C.   VARIABLES SETTING

To develop a longitudinal analysis, it is necessary, according to Toon Taris, to standardize the use of dependent and independent variables within the study. This is possible in this case because the Mexican government adopted the same approach the U.S. has been using for more than 40 years in its war on drugs (Brownfield, 2011a). According to Luis Astorga, this approach is based on attacking transnational organized crime at its production and transit sites, instead of addressing consumption inside the U.S. (Astorga, 2010).

To perform such a task, it was necessary to identify variables such as the U.S. interest in immigration, politics, economics, and drug trafficking, and turn them into separate research factors, due to their particularly relevant role in Mexican homeland security.

The identification and further analysis of the dependent and independent variables allow us to understand why Mexico is the weak link in Pan-American security and also explain why events such as fighting among the cartels is a token that this pattern is changing.

14

Based on the August 2011, Mitofsky's poll, the current state of knowledge about the Mexican problem represents a gap in understanding. According to this poll, in August 2011, 60 percent of Mexicans thought Mexico was heading in the wrong direction (Campos, 2011), 36.6 percent thought that security was the worst problem, 75 percent approve of the armed forces, and 65 percent approve of the government. It seems clear that, even when part of the Mexican population thinks the cartels are winning the war on drugs, the society trusts its institutions (Campos, 2011). In contrast, according to information released by the Mexican government in June 2011, 90 percent of the 45,000 casualties to date are cartel members; five percent belong to the armed and police forces, and five percent are civilians (CNN, 2010).

D.   HYPOTHESES

Mexico's geopolitical location has created a homeland disadvantage in terms of the Pan-American security chain. Its proximity to the U.S. and its condition as a developing country could turn Mexico as the weakest link in the Americas' security chain. However, this path is changing notably, because Mexico sent the pressure back to U.S. by asking for assistance to support its strategy.

If this argument is true, we can make three preliminary conclusions: first, the Mexican strategy against transnational organized crime has been successful; second, Mexico is no longer the weakest link in the Americas security chain; and third, the narco-traffic problem will migrate to another region in Latin America.

The variables established to test the hypothesis are the balloon effect over Mexico's territory (a dependent variable) and strategies developed by the government (independent variables). The constant variables are criminal organizations and their activities, because they are the target of the strategies and will be used as measure of effectiveness.

If the number of cartel leaders, cartels, or cartel members, drugs, prices, or routes, varies across the cases included in the analysis, then the strategy is giving positive outcomes; by contrast, the Mexican strategy could be considered as a failure if the criminal organizations recover their stability inside Mexico because the government abandons the effort.

This design and structure comprise the theoretical framework of this thesis.

E. METHODOLOGY

The longitudinal case study is conducted based on three cases where some U.S. strategies have created balloon effects in Mexico. The cases were selected based on the premise that they are an integral part of a bigger research strategy necessary to determine whether Mexico has been affected by the balloon effects of macro strategies with positive or negative outcomes.

The research was made using open, primary, and secondary sources. The primary sources are government documents. Information gathered from secondary sources was cross-checked for consistency. The use of data such as preferences of the population, based on polls, is limited; however, the data is supported from a variety of different studies and articles.

Other alternative strategies were considered during case selection to reinforce impartiality and counterbalance the bias towards suspicion regarding the tendencies of a finding, such as concerning the Colombia plan. However, they were not included in the study because it is focused mainly in the relationship between México and the U.S.

In order to develop a "structure and focused comparison" (George & Bennett, 2005), it was necessary to standardize relevant data from specific cases. One instance is that the strategies were chosen without looking at political affiliations.

Following the logic of the theory proposed by Gorge and Bennett, and to give the same outline to the cases, we immerse ourselves in the chronological narrative of the cases, establishing the criterion for dependent and independent variables, and how they would be used to score from a positive or negative perspective and establish reliability. Consequently, the cases were chosen in chronological order and for different balloon effects. In the last case, we will analyze the balloon effects of a Mexican strategy inside Mexico and the balloon effects of counter-pressure inside the U.S.

This thesis used theoretical and empirical information to develop the longitudinal case study and reach its theoretical conclusion. Since the findings have not been tested, they must be considered provisional. To be considered in the development of future theories or strategies, they must first be reassessed and reconsidered, following a more focused approach. Second, they must be challenged by other analysis using the same hypothesis and variables in order either to reach a different point of view about the Mexican situation or support thesis findings.

In conclusion, strengthening the historical relevance of the strategies selected will test our hypotheses about the main concern of this thesis, which is to see the current Mexican government's strategy from a different perspective, invalidating the misunderstood point of a failed strategy.

F.   RESEARCH PROBLEM

Late 2006, when Calderon came to power, Mexico was living in a relatively calm situation. According to Mitofsky's poll conducted in April 2010, the main concerns among Mexican society were in the social arena, rather than security (Campos, 2010).

Problems before 2006 included a high rate of kidnapping and robbery in places like Morelos, Guerrero, and Michoacán, which had the highest national index of crime according to the 2006 Congressional Report on Criminology (Reyes Tépach, 2006).

According to the same report, the national criminality index appeared to be growing. This trend forced Calderon´s administration to change its pre-campaign pledges from labor to security (Presidencia de la Republica Mexicana, 2007b).

In February 2007, Calderon´s administration implemented high-impact operations against transnational organized crime to recover the spaces they were occupying (Presidencia de la Republica Mexicana, 2007b), creating local operations in cities such as Matamoros, Ciudad Juarez, Tijuana, Acapulco, and Cuernavaca (Presidencia de la Republica Mexicana, 2007a).

17

As a consequence of this strategy, the entire Mexican crime structure was unbalanced, showing balloon effects in terms of a sudden rise of violence in those places where the armed forces were policing the streets.

At the same time, the Mexican government asked for U.S. support to confront a bigger security problem, one directly related to drugs (U.S. State Department, 2009; United States Government Accountability Office, 2010).

Consequently, in October 2007, the governments of Mexico, the U.S., the nations of Central America, the Dominican Republic, and Haiti, developed the "Merida Initiative," a multinational strategy created to confront criminal organizations whose illicit actions undermined public safety, eroded the rule of law, and threatened the national security of the countries involved.

It was within this framework that the research problem for this thesis was formulated, trying to answer complex questions such as why, though not a drug-consuming country itself, Mexico is suffering the consequences of transnational organized crime mainly focus on the drug business. Could this systemic behavior be illuminated following the logic of scientific analysis? What is the point of intervention that alters the stability of a system? What is influencing Mexican society's perception of a failed strategy? How can this idea be changed? And finally, what measures of effectiveness and proficiency can be established to evaluate the strategic success?

Although the data's preliminary observations suggest negative results, it was obvious that the strategy must have had positive intentions reflecting in its policy decisions.

III. LONGITUDINAL CASE STUDY

A. INTRODUCTION

The main intention of this longitudinal analysis is to examine the balloon effect of three strategies developed in the Western Hemisphere by the U.S., and their implications in the security field in Mexico. The purpose is to determine, using the balloon-effect hypothesis, whether Mexico's geopolitical location makes it the weakest link in the Pan-American security chain and the natural recipient of second-order effects coming from the strategies selected.

According to the International Monetary Fund, the Americas have two of the "advanced economies" of the world; however, it also has Latin America, considered "emerging and/or developing economies" (International Monetary Fund, 2011).

From this geopolitical perspective, Mexico geopolitical location could be considered the representation of the Americas' false dichotomy; Mexico is the southernmost, less-developed country of North America and also the northernmost country of Latin America, with the highest gross domestic product.

In other words, Mexico is the geographical link between the North America advanced economies, or commonly known as "developed economies," and Latin America, also known as developing, or "third world countries."

As a consequence of this proximity disadvantage, every time Mexico interacts with its North American partners, it acts as the weakest link in the Pan-American security chain. Paradoxically, the same logic applies when Mexico has to interact with other countries in Latin America supported by U.S., due to the fact that Mexico has to interact, indirectly, with U.S. power, confronting once again the impact of balloon effects and rendering Mexico the weakest link in the "interdependent security ecosystem" (Ulieru, 2008).

19

Mihaela Ulieru's article states that the interdependence of security ecosystems makes twenty-first century threats different from those in the past, and creates the need to develop means of interaction among involved organizations, such as military interaction, to achieve a common goal (Ulieru, 2008).

Rewording Ulieru's approach, we can say that the interdependent security ecosystem drives governments to evaluate options for regional threats according to each actor's capacities.

The cases included in this longitudinal analysis are the U.S.'s 1882 Chinese-Exclusion Act, 1969 Operation Intercept, and 1994 North America Free-Trade Agreement. These cases are developed at the strategic level of analysis because they were conceived at the strategic level under a macro vision; their balloon effects reflected at the macro level in terms of politics, yet had implications at the meso and micro level of analysis inside Mexico, confirming the impact of the balloon effect within Mexican homeland security.

Other cases, such as Plan Colombia, or the Caribbean Basin Initiative, could also be included in this type of analysis because they created balloon effects in Mexican homeland security as well (Griffith, 1997; Meiners, 2009). Such was clearly the case in the Colombia Plan and consequent resurgence of the Mexican cartels in the early 2000s (Correspondent, 2010; Fieser, 2010). However, these cases were excluded because the goal of this thesis is to analyze the balloon effects and their repercussions over the Mexican homeland at the meso and micro level of analysis, as well as balloon-effect counter-pressure from the Mexican strategy against transnational organized crime.

B.   THE U.S. CHINESE-EXCLUSION ACT: 1882

I am not born for one corner; the whole world is my native land...

Seneca the Younger (4 BC–64 AD)

1.   Background

The Chinese are upon us. How can we get rid of them? The Chinese are coming. How can we stop them...?

(Craig, 1980)

According to Richard Craig, these were the concerns about Chinese immigration to America voiced in 1876 by H. N. Clement before the California state senate, leading to the creation of the committee for the investigation of the "social, moral, and political effects" of Chinese immigration in California (Craig, 1980). According to Gaston Pardo, a Mexican sociologist, Clements's testimony was intended to reach, not only a local, but a national audience for creating a strong movement against the Chinese who immigrated during the California Gold Rush (Pardo, 2008).

Promotion of the law was based on the argument that the Chinese who came during 1848–1885 were threatening the American population in California after the end of the Gold Rush, contributing to job scarcity and deficiency. According to Richard Craig, the anti-Chinese movement started at the community, then the state, and later the national, level, as locals encouraged the U.S. Congress to create and pass an act to curtail Chinese immigration and protect the American interest.

According to Julia Schiavone Camacho (2009), it was years later, when efforts made by U.S. citizens against Chinese immigration proved successful, that the United States Congress passed the Chinese-Exclusion Act on May 6, 1882, signed by President Chester A. Arthur (1881–1885). This document is considered the first U.S. law against an ethnic group (Schiavone Camacho, 2009). Camacho and Craig agree that Chinese laborers were targeted by the law, with the argument that they were endangering U.S. communities, especially in California. The law excluded Chinese from immigration and naturalization for a period of 10 years, with the exception of merchants, teachers, students, travelers, and diplomats, confirming the law's bias against Chinese laborers (Craig, 1980; Schiavone Camacho, 2009).

Reviewing the 16 sections of restrictions included in the act, we can confirm why just a few Chinese could pass muster and enter the country at that time, and why those already in transit had to change their destination. Some of the enforcing mechanisms of the law required the Chinese to reregister with the U.S. government and rearrange their certificate of residence. If they could not meet the new requirement, which was almost certain, they would be required to leave the country or face deportation. The law required the Chinese to start the certification process almost immediately after passage, with no other option than to go back to China or migrate elsewhere if they could not meet legal requirements (United States Government, 1882).

This alternative was Mexico. And the opportunity was opened on the other side of the U.S. border by the Mexican president, Porfírio Díaz (1787–1880; 1884–1911). Diaz was trying to modernize the country, building railroads to connect the slightly populated northern states with the rest of the country—which created labor opportunities (Curtis, 1995; Pardo, 2008). According to Pardo, this government enterprise was the catalyst for U.S. subcontractors and many persons facing the Chinese-Exclusion Act to change their residency from the U.S. to Mexico, change their destination to Mexico if they were already in transit to the U.S., or emigrate to Mexico explicitly to build the railroads (2008).

In terms of the systems-thinking theory presented by Anderson, and Johnson the Mexican government's window of opportunity was a "point of leverage" (Anderson & Johnson, 1997) for the system in favor to the Chinese people, giving them the opportunity to enter the country and creating a positive balloon effect for México.

However, though Chinese people are now embedded in Mexican society, their process of adaptation lasted decades. Authors such as Joe Cummings (2001), Richard Craig (1980), and James Curtis (1995) mention the perils that the Chinese confronted in order to escape from the U.S. to Mexico. Joe Cummings, in his article "Mexicali's

22

Chinatown: Shark-Fish Tacos and Barbecue Chow Mein," discusses the deaths of 160 Chinese trying to cross the San Felipe Desert at the crossroad of La Trinidad, named "The Chinese" due to the enormous transit in the area and as a memorial to those who lost their lives in that enterprise (Cummings, 2001). As mentioned in the introduction, however, migration considered solely cannot be regarded as a balloon effect coming from the Chinese-Exclusion Act; the balloon effects would be the second-order effects caused by the Chinese people as a consequence of their migration.

Following hydraulics and chemistry and applying, we can say that flows can be stable from the molecular point of view, yet not static by nature. This means that, once in motion, a flow will tend to remain in motion because of inertia. Applying this metaphor to the consequences of the Chinese-Exclusion Act, Mexico can be considered the weak link in the security chain because the Chinese people chose Mexico from among other countries as their destination.

The Chinese had to find the best way to fit within the new system in Mexico. The closest and easiest way to enter Mexico was by crossing the California border. Once in Mexico, the Chinese settled along the northern states, such as Baja California and Sonora, where they brought positive contribution (Pardo, 2008). This can be considered a positive influence of the balloon effect in those places where Chinese people arrived. Julia Schiavone and Buchenau Jürgen mention that initially hundreds, later thousands, of Chinese arrived in places like Mexicali, starting small business such as restaurants and laundries (Buchenau, 2001; Schiavone Camacho, 2009).

Paradoxically, as Jose Cummings notes, during the U.S. Prohibition years (1920–1933), Chinese people recovered a relevant position in the northern Mexican border cities. According to Cummings:

> When Americans flocked to Mexican border towns to partake of the alcoholic beverages outlawed at home, Chinese laborers and farmers moved into the Mexican cities and spent their hard-earned savings not only to open bars, restaurants, and hotels but also to establish an underground tunnel system connecting both sides of the border with the purpose of trafficking drugs and alcohol.

This activity can be considered destiny's revenge. According to Cummings, "Many, but by no means all, of the prohibition-era Mexican businesses over the border were operated by Chinese people" (2001); this behavior was a negative balloon effect of Chinese immigration to Mexico.

Camacho and Curtis cite the Mexican Revolution (1910–1920) as the reason the Mexican government did not take action against illegal business in the northern border, arguing that the government was busy fighting the revolution. At the end of the revolution, the new Mexican government became aware of the sudden rise of casinos and prostitution rings in northern Mexico, as well as direct Chinese implication in these businesses. Unfortunately for the Chinese people, the government turned the situation into another anti-Chinese movement, this time within Mexico (Curtis, 1995; Schiavone Camacho, 2009).

The government's "point of intervention" (Anderson & Johnson, 1997) resulted in the prosecution, torture, and murder of hundreds of Chinese (Schiavone Camacho, 2009). However, one significant difference between the two unfortunate events, according to Curtis, was that the Mexican government did not reject immigration nor deny Mexican citizenship to the Chinese people (Curtis, 1995).

According to Camacho, during the Mexican anti-Chinese movement, some Mexican regions, specifically Baja California, became a haven for Chinese running away from the violence on both sides of the border. As a humanitarian act, in early 1940's the Mexican government changed its national policies, allowing legal Chinese immigration in the country (Schiavone Camacho, 2009).

The establishment of the Chinese people and their enrollment in Mexican society in northern Mexico can be considered a component of the balloon effect, based on the fact that Chinese influence had secondary consequences in that particular region of the country. Consequently, we can discern the weakest link of the system not only at the macro but also at the meso and micro levels of analysis.

When we talk about the macro level, it does not matter whether we are talking about hundreds of miles or just one; the target's having crossed an international border implies the macro level of analysis. Consequently, because the Chinese people migrated from California to Baja California, we must refer to the macro level of analysis. Getting deep in to the meso and micro levels of analysis, we can say that the balloon effects were reflected in the northern region, where Chinese people settled due to the proximity to the border. Following the logic of Mihaela Ulieru's "interdependent security ecosystem," we can conclude that those cities that received the impact of the Chinese-Exclusion Act, represented at the meso and micro level of analysis the weakest link in the Mexican security chain.

Traces of the Mexican Chinese migration can be found all over the country. Nowadays one can find Catholic Chinese descendants with names such as "Guadalupe," who are as Mexican as other native Mexicans (Schiavone Camacho, 2009), eating and cooking Mexican-Chinese food and generally showing how well embedded they are in the population (Cummings, 2001).

Consequently, the Chinese presence and influence spreads at the meso and micro levels inside Mexico up to the point where Chinese communities are found anywhere, in states such as Chiapas, Sonora, Mexico City, and Baja California. Instance of this migration is Mexicali, Baja California, largest Chinese community in the country, followed by Mexico City, and Tapachula, Chiapas (Schiavone Camacho, 2009).

The reason the Chinese choose Mexico instead of Canada, or the state of Baja California, or Chiapas instead of Coahuila, or Mexicali instead of Tijuana or Ensenada (which are only a few miles apart), can be considered the signs of Mexican weakness in this North American region. It may possibly be considered a sign of weakness at the national and local level of analysis as well; however, from the Mexican perspective, whether the current influence of the Chinese population is negative or positive in terms of the balloon effect cannot be determined.

The most important part of the history is the win–win situation created by the beneficial interaction of Mexican and Chinese culture, which helped the early process of Mexican modernization. According to Jürgen Buchenau and Curtis, Chinese immigrants seized control of banking and commerce; today, Chinese people play an important role in the Mexican academy, arts, and national politics (Buchenau, 2001), giving them the opportunity to attain a better way of life and monetary success (Curtis, 1995).

2.   Conclusion

The Chinese-Exclusion Act was a unilateral American strategy targeting the Chinese population's influence in California communities. As a result of pressure on the Chinese people within or in transit to the U.S., there was a flow of displaced persons over the U.S.–Mexican border. The balloon effects of that migration, according to Julia Schiavone Camacho, James Curtis, Jürgen Buchenau, have been positive for the Mexican economy and population (Buchenau, 2001; Curtis, 1995; Schiavone Camacho, 2009). Though this interaction was not necessarily easy for the Chinese or the Mexicans, today there is relative calm in terms of ethnic-Chinese to Mexico (Cummings, 2001; Payan, 2006).

In conclusion, the 1882 U.S. Chinese-Exclusion Act created a balloon effect inside Mexico, not only at the macro, but also at meso and micro levels of analysis. Fortunately, the aftermath of the case can be considered positive for all: the native population, the Chinese immigrants, and finally, for the U.S. population and government who passed the Chinese-Exclusion Act.

The law did not cause any apparent inconvenience to the U.S. and may be deemed a successful strategy. Therefore no balloon-effect counter-pressure can be attributed to the Act.

Mexico, as the recipient of the balloon effects of the Chinese-Exclusion Act, particularly in the northern region, turned to be the weakest link in the security chain, not only at the macro, but also at the meso and micro level.

C.   OPERATION INTERCEPT: 1969

The nation, which indulges towards another an habitual hatred, or and habitual fondness, is in some degree a slave. It is a slave to its animosity or to its affection, either of which is sufficient to lead it astray from its duty and its interest.

George Washington

1.   Background (Twelve Days)

In contrast to the shortness of the introductory phrase, the importance of America's Operation Intercept rests in the huge number of second-order balloon effects, not only on the strategy's target, Mexico, but also at the micro, meso, and macro levels of analysis. It is important also because this strategy caused balloon-effect counter-pressure inside the U.S. at the economic, social, and political levels.

Applying the balloon-effect concept, we will analyze if Mexico received the secondary effects of Operation Intercept, thus confirming the theory of migration of the target from the place of pressure to the weakest point inside the system.

Operation Intercept is the name of a unilateral U.S. operation launched from September 21 to October 2, 1969, along the U.S.–Mexican border (Lawrence, 1974). The overt purpose of this operation was to interdict the flow of marijuana and other drugs into the U.S. The covert intention of Nixon's administration, according to Richard Craig, was to force the Mexican government into more active participation in the war on drugs (Craig, 1980).

Craig, an expert on Operation Intercept, also states that the initial intention of the U.S. government was "a lifetime operation;" in contrast, Operation Intercept lasted just 12 days due to immense secondary effects (Craig, 1980).

2.   The Balloon Effects of a Public Policy

According to Robert Deitch, who wrote his book, *Hemp: American History Revisited* six years after Operation Intercept's conclusion, one of Nixon's strongest promises during its 1968 presidential campaign was to take action against drug consumption (Deitch, 2003). Consequently, when he came to power, he had no other option but to face America's staggering national drug-abuse problem. In his "Special Message to the Congress on Control of Narcotics and Dangerous Drugs" on July 14, 1969, Nixon cited the importance of the problem right up front in his opening statement: "Within the last decade, the abuse of drugs has grown from essentially a local police problem to a serious national threat, to the personal and safety of millions of Americans" (Nixon, 1969). Nixon created an interdepartmental task force: first, "to conduct a comprehensive study of the marijuana issue, with specific emphasis on the Mexican border," and second, to developed a strategy for a "positive and effective action to control the illicit trafficking of drugs across the Mexican border" (Nixon, 1969). Synthesizing Craig's words, the problem was marijuana, the target, Mexico (Craig, 1980).

According to Craig's investigations, the task force began its commitment by gathering and examining empirical and factual evidence about American drug abuse. One of the commission's first findings was a relationship between drug use (particularly marijuana), deterioration in user health, and increase in crime (Craig, 1980). The commission established the relationship between drug trafficking and Mexico in order to target the Mexican border.

As a consequence of these findings, the task force produced a document entitled "Report of Special Presidential Task Force Relating to Narcotics, Marijuana and Dangerous Drugs" released on June 6, 1969 (Interdepartmental Task Force, 1969). Almost a month later, in an address to Congress, President Nixon addressed two concerns from the task force's preliminary report. First, that Mexico is the primary source of almost all of the marijuana seized in the United States, and second, that increased reports about the use of marijuana in the middle and high schools, with no distinction between public and private schools, raised the problem to the national concern (Nixon, 1969). According to Craig, the most troubling situation pointed out by the commission was the growing evidence of pre-teenagers using marijuana (Craig, 1980). This chaotic situation can explain why Nixon ordered a "high priority frontal attack" on border trafficking (Nixon, 1969).

According to Craig's investigation and analysis, performed almost 10 years later, Nixon's initial instructions to the commission showed a slight awareness of the possible

28

political implications, based on the content of a letter in which Nixon mentioned that the Mexican ambassador to "would be posted" about the operation (1991). Closing the loop during previous meetings, the commission had reported that "they [the commission] will be working closely with the Mexican government" (Craig, 1991).

Unfortunately, these actions mentioned by President Nixon were never accomplished. The Mexican government was not informed about the operation, and the ambassador was not asked to work with the commission, provoking important secondary effects in both countries.

Operation Intercept tried to tackle the drug problem in three ways: in the short term by reducing the amount of marijuana coming from Mexico into the United States; in the midterm by creating a market scarcity of drugs, with repercussions on the price; and finally, in the long term, and as a direct result of the first two actions, a reduction in illegal usage (Interdepartmental Task Force, 1969).

According to Craig's article "Operation Intercept," the U.S. government ordered a huge mobilization of manpower and economic resources along the Mexican border, as well as legal actions. The Federal Aviation Administration (FAA) imposed restrictions and requirement for all civilian pilots flying to or from Mexico; the U.S. Navy put Tijuana "off limits" to all military personnel; and finally, the U.S. imposed secrecy surrounding the upcoming blockade to Mexico (Craig, 1980).

During Operation Intercept's initial stage, 18 points of entry were tested along the border, with an initial estimated cost of $30,000,000 USD (Craig, 1980). According to Craig, John Ingersoll, former director of the Bureau of Narcotics and Dangerous Drugs, mentioned that Operation Intercept was "a very high monetary price for a single operation" (Craig, 1980). In an earlier article, Lawrence Gooberman established that the measures of effectiveness were not just the cost versus benefit over the national population, but also the desired secondary effects expected in the diplomatic arena (1974).

In order to enlist Mexico's direct participation as a complement in the American war on drugs, the U.S. government focused its approach on production sites and in-route countries—and Mexico fit both (Fowler, 1996).

We must analyze the information presented before we can conclude that there was a clear consciousness about possible second-order effects to Mexico of Operation Intercept. But clearly, what decision makers did not consider was the balloon-effect counter-pressure inside the U.S.

Craig and Fowler agree that immediately upon the implementation of the operation, the daily life of thousands of locals on the Mexican side of the border started to feel the change, most notably in rough new border-crossing procedures. Not only shoppers, tourists, school children, and university students, but also green-card workers trying cross the border as usual arrived late to their duties. Others chose to stay home instead of wasting time "making the line" (Fowler, 1996; Gooberman, 1974). In this sense, if we consider local disturbances and their political implications in both sides of the border, we can conclude that the strategy had remarkable success and also that government has the capacity to create balloon effects on purpose. Paraphrasing Gooberman, Operation Intercept reached its desired balloon effect by turning border communities upside down, forcing the Mexican government and society to react to the strategy (Gooberman, 1974).

The thousands of inspections that took place over the 18 checkpoints along the border represent pressure on the balloon; the tensions at the local level were the desired balloon effects. The most remarkable success in terms of desired balloon effects is what Craig cited in his article, "Operation Intercept: The International Politics of Pressure," which is about the embarrassing outrage of September 23, when the Mexican consul general in El Paso, Robert S. Urrea, was rudely searched while trying to cross the Juarez–El Paso border (Craig, 1980). Based on this lack of diplomatic courtesy, the Mexican government escalated the incident and sent the Mexican foreign minister to meet with his U.S. counterpart at United Nations headquarters. Craig also mentioned that:

> The Mexican minister asserted before the assembly that '[I am] acting
> under precise presidential instruction,' adding that '[We] respected the

competency of the U.S. authorities to pursue the methods they deem opportune over their territory and population,' and that 'if [these] methods affect the Mexican territory and population, it is necessary for [us] to let [U.S. authorities] know it.'

Craig's analysis is correct in terms of the covert intention of Operation Intercept and its desired second-order consequences; however, we can add that by reacting in that particular way, the Mexican government was sending the appropriate signal to the U.S. government about the strategy's success.

From the American perspective, and aside from those desired and undesired balloon effects, Operation Intercept was in some fashion positive. According to United States Customs, the supply of marijuana coming from Mexico was noticeable reduced during Operation Intercept (Deitch, 2003). According to Robert Deitch's *Hemp: An American History Revisited*, according to the local news in places like Los Angeles, New York, and Chicago, when the drug was available, the prices doubled and in some cases tripled (2003). Unfortunately, the same information gathered by Deitch showed that this tactical success was momentary because the marijuana scarcity created a balloon-effect counter-pressure in favor of the importation of other drugs, such as heroin and hashish, and the emergence of new synthetic drugs such as barbiturates, barbituric acids, and amphetamines (Craig, 1980; Deitch, 2003). The scarcity of marijuana coming from abroad also incentivized the local cultivation of marijuana in states like Chicago.

Trying to justify Operation Intercept, Vernon D. Meyer, Deputy Regional Director of the U.S. Bureau of Narcotics and Dangerous Drugs, said that the imported marijuana jumped from about $200 to $400 a kilogram and that domestic marijuana remained at about $200 a kilogram (Gooberman, 1974). According to the local police in cities such as Los Angeles and New York, drug consumption did not reduce substantially and the cost of the marijuana on the streets did not increase substantially (Craig 1980). Comparing the statistics, Craig (1980) considered that the strategy, in terms of the cost versus benefits of drug seizure, was not worth it. Thomas Fowler, in his book *The International Narcotics Trade: Can it be Stopped by Interdiction*, states that the interdiction of drugs by itself is not effective (1996) and proposes a holistic approach to the problem.

Another balloon effect in terms of behavior was the October 1, 1969, "Operation Dignity," an economic buy-at-home campaign initiated by the Mexican border community with the purpose of affecting business on the U.S. side. According to the *Modesto* [California] *Bee* newspaper, this action by the Mexican Chamber of Commerce expressed a desire to force the U.S. to modify or terminate its unilateral strategy (Mexicans Launched Operation Dignity, 1969).

Paradoxically to the positive expected outcomes, paraphrasing Craig, the U.S. society wondered about the strategy's real cost versus benefit, comparing the U.S. government's achievements in terms of the operation's measures of effectiveness in term of drug's trafficking reduction and consumption among the youth (Craig, 1980).

In examining the cost versus benefit of Operation Intercept, we can determine that the official goal was to take action against the U.S. drug consumption, in response to societal demand. However, since the balloon effects over the border divided American society, not only at the local and national, but also at the international level, the program's counter-pressures swung the balance towards Operation Intercept's cancellation, with the final decision resting with President Nixon.

According to Craig, the influential U.S.–Mexico Borders Cities Association, followed by the local business community, filed a complaint asking the government to reconsider procedures and to downgrade inspections to the status of spot checks. Craig also pointed out that the Hawaiian senator Daniel Inouye described the maneuver as "the worst diplomatic blunder" of the decade," encouraging the president to admit that they were wrong and to publicly apologize to Mexico (Craig, 1991). In his investigation 10 years after the program, Craig reaffirms that the architects of Operation Intercept, in their "headlong" rush to achieve immediate, spectacular results, simply lacked what Peter Schwartz would called "the art of the long view" (Schwartz, 1996).

3.   Operation Intercept's Balloon Effects

As previously mentioned, Operation Intercept's balloon effects, whether desired and undesired, had political implications. One of these came directly from the highest level of the Mexican government (Doyle, 2011). In the ceremony dedicating the new

Amistad Dam, Mexican President Gustavo Diaz Ordaz declared that Mexico, especially the northern states and border communities, were badly affected by Operation Intercept's balloon effects. Coincidently, this message was given by the Mexican president first, along the Texas–Coahuila border (Craig, 1980). Kate Doyle (2011), in her article "Operation Intercept the Perils of Unilateralism," notes that when Nixon was preparing to meet Díaz Ordaz for the ceremony:

> His National Security Advisor Henry Kissinger pointed this out in his secret briefing paper to Nixon just days before the ceremony [that] 'The meeting at Amistad Dam is important because it will demonstrate the continuation of the close and constructive relations which exist between the United States and Mexico.'

Other important advice given to Nixon, according to Doyle, was to not give Diaz Ordaz any specific warning about the operation (Doyle, 2011).

Nonetheless, the desired second-order, balloon effect expected from Operation Intercept arrived better sooner than later. According to Lawrence Gooberman, few days after the conclusion of the operation, government officials from both countries started discussions about switching the approach (1974). Considering the reserved Operation Intercept opening in September 21, 1969, and the desired and undesired balloon effects, we can say that the strategy did reach one of its objectives: in a bilateral conference, officials from both countries announced that "a mutual understanding prevailed, based on the good relationship between the U.S. and Mexico" (Brownfield, 2011c). Consequently, in a concerted decision, "Operation Intercept" was superseded while a mutual agreement was reached, opening the "Operation Cooperation" era (Craig, 1980; Gooberman, 1974).

Two months later, in a conclusion to this political episode, Nixon personally apologized to the Diaz Ordaz for Operation Intercept's balloon effects, as follows (Craig, 1974):

> Mr. President, I want to express my personal regret for the friction which Operation Intercept has caused in the relations between our two countries. Operation Intercept was conceived as one element in a major campaign to combat the traffic in narcotics from whatever source. It was not intended to single out Mexico, or to give offense to Mexico. I want to give you my personal assurances on this point. When it became apparent to me that this

operation was being viewed, by your Government as an affront to the Mexican people, I asked that the intensity of the inspections be reduced to a point where the major frictions and irritations which the operation had caused in our relations with Mexico could be eliminated.

4. Conclusion

Due to its enormous balloon effects and subsequent counter-pressure, Operation Intercept is not a common topic of conversation in U.S.–Mexican circles. However, its fallout is reflected in the relationship between the two countries, influencing many government policies.

Operation Intercept started at the micro level of analysis, from a local political decision, yet, its concept of operations escalated its repercussions to the macro level, due to intended and unintended balloon effects internationally. Nevertheless, Operation Intercept started the unilateral U.S. approach to an antidrug policy, or "war on drugs."

Even though Operation Intercept did not reach its tactical goal with regard to the reduction of drug abuse, it reached its desired second-order effect, of securing Mexican involvement in the war on drugs—contrary to what Whitworth mentioned about the balloon effects as a consequence of "tactical successes and strategic failures" (2008).

Craig (1974) argues that Operation Intercept uncovered empirical and theoretical information concerning the behavior of the transnational, organized-crime business model. It also unveiled considerable factual information about the balloon effects of implementing a unilateral strategy in the international arena.

In terms of the Americas' security chain, the balloon effects of the unilateral Operation Intercept reinforce the hypothesis of Mexico as the weakest link in the Pan-American security chain, due to the fact that the U.S. considered provoking Mexico's reaction while causing chaos over the border, showing its unilateral influence over Mexico. This point is also made by Doyle (2011).

The undesired balloon-effects counter-pressure inside the U.S. shows the importance of developing a comprehensive strategic plan (Mintzber, 1994; Schwartz,

1996). It also demonstrates the contrary effects of ignoring it and facing what Mintzberg et al. called "the wilds of strategic management," that is, being reactive in order to reach short-term objectives (1998).

Analyzing Nixon's letter to Díaz Ordaz, "Operation Intercept was conceived as one element in a major campaign to combat the traffic in narcotics from whatever source" (Nixon, 1969) can be interpreted to mean that getting Mexico's involvement was the main purpose of Operation Intercept, and not drug interdiction at the border. As Craig concluded, the point was "to inflict pressure over Mexico through economic denial seeking a politically expedite solution to the highly complex problem of domestic drug abuse" (Craig, 1980).

Therefore, while Intercept proved a short- and intermediate-term diplomatic blunder, it indirectly became the long-term catalyst to improving the Mexican antidrug campaign, as well as a springboard to more effective U.S. cooperation.

As a corollary to this operation, can say that the cooperation between the Mexican and American governments has improved over the years. Maybe the most valuable balloon effect of the strategy is the fact that Operation Intercept opened a more inclusive way of developing strategies between the two nations.

D.   NORTH AMERICA FREE TRADE AGREEMENT: 1994

> . . . *Treaties, which are not built upon reciprocal benefits, are not likely to be of long duration.*

George Washington

> *'We have to understand North America as a shared economic space,'* one that *'we need to protect. . .'*

Under-Secretary of State Thomas Shannon

1.   Background

In 1988, when Mexican President Carlos Salinas de Gortari came in power, expectations about Mexico's future were high around the world. With a degree in economic policies from Harvard University, Salinas was considered a radical reformer

(Crandall, Paz, & Roett, 2005; Teichman, 2001). Using his experiences as the Mexican Minister of Budget and Programming (Secretario de Programación y Presupuesto), Salinas implemented aggressive government policies privatizing state-owned enterprises and opening the national industry to foreign competition, trying to push Mexico into the globalized world. According to Laura Carlsen, and Fefeer, NAFTA presented an opportunity for the Bush administration "to create more advantageous conditions for transnational corporations and remove remaining barriers to the flow of capital and cross-border production" (Carlsen & Fefeer, 2007). NAFTA was a strategy conceived under two different perspectives, the Mexican and the American, in an effort to improve the economies of both countries.

Based on its design, we can deduce that when NAFTA was signed on January 1, 1994, few people thought about its security implications. From the Mexican perspective, only some organizations such as the Zapatistas guerrilla movement were interested, having used NAFTA as an issue to underline Mexico's disadvantages in terms of monetary resources (Clio, 2002). Some environmentalist organizations raised questions about the exploitation of natural resources, reinforcing the Zapatista's claim, and the industrial-waste pollution caused by the U.S. in some border regions, demanding that NAFTA be modified in favor of better trade for Mexico (Arrollo, 2003).

In her book, *The Politics of Freeing Markets in Latin America: Chile, Argentina, and Mexico*, Judith Teichman offers political reasons for U.S. impediments to NAFTA, which hindered broad improvements while waiting for congressional approval (2001).

But things change, and disastrous events such as September 11, 2001, provided a different framework to NAFTA. After the 9/11 terrorist attacks, President George W. Bush (2001–2009) launched the U.S. war on terrorism, based on his 2002 national-security strategy. Bush's priorities turned to homeland security, including the borders. According to the Congressional Research Service 2010 report to Congress, there is a possibility that some terrorist organizations were trying to establish links with Mexican cartels to smuggle illegal materials over the border, and narcotraffic methods are cited (Rollins, Wyler, & Rosen, 2010). As a consequence of the war on terrorism, the Bush administration sought to protect the susceptible and vulnerable U.S. society by using

NAFTA as a platform to create a trilateral integration model called the Security and Prosperity Partnership of North America—a complement to, but not part of, NAFTA.

2.   The Openness Paradox

The link between terrorist groups and criminal organizations is considered by Dennis Bayle (2005) in his book, *The Openness Society Paradox*. According to Bayle, American society is so open, so free, that terrorist as well as criminal organizations can use that freedom to perpetrate acts against the American people (Bayle, 2005). The outcomes of Bayle's openness paradox can be considered in terms of the balloon effect of undesired secondary effects. According to Bayle, U.S. openness was one of the contributing factors to 9/11 because "the openness of American society has left the U.S. susceptible as well as vulnerable to today's threats." This includes terrorism as well as transnational, organized-crime activities.

The linking point in how NAFTA could be improved in the security field can be found in the 2002 National Security Strategy: "In our own hemisphere, we will advance the vision of a free trade area of the Americas by building on the North American Free Trade Agreement." Analyzing those words, we can discover the outline for the Security and Prosperity Partnership of North America (SPP), NAFTA's complement in the security field. The purpose of SPP is to create cooperation on security and economic issues in North America, trying to contain what we call balloon effects from NAFTA's openness paradox.

Under-Secretary of State Thomas Shannon, introducing the SPP on March 2005, declared that North America must be understood as a shared economic space, one that needed protection—adding that, to a certain extent, they were armoring NAFTA.

The three independent SPP websites agree that SPP was created because prosperity is dependent on security; however, even when the program recognizes that the great nations of Canada, America, and Mexico "share a belief in freedom, economic opportunity, and strong democratic institutions," it does not consider the imbalance of power among them, which makes Mexico the weakest link in the security chain of North America. Reinforcing this argument, we have to consider the information presented by the Heritage Foundation's 2011 index of economic freedom. The United States is ranked ninth freest nation in the world; Canada is ranked sixth; and Mexico lags far behind in forty-eighth place (International Monetary Fund, 2011).

In the SPP initial statement, "harmonizing" the simplification of trade procedures and the creation of more unified norms and standards (U.S. Department of State, 2005) is a recurring theme. The norms seek to make easier for U.S. companies to ship production overseas, eliminating Mexican and Canadian labor. In terms of security from the U.S. perspective, "harmonization" means harsher security measures, without considering the balloon effects such as those of Operation Intercept back in 1969. By contrast, for Mexico, harmonization means to implement processes to reach U.S. requirements, taking in consideration its less-developed status.

3.   Solutions to the Openness Paradox Included in Security and Prosperity Partnership of North America

One of the central points concerning border-management policies in the SPP is how to facilitate the efficient entry of legal cargo, while hindering the illegal, and affording a sufficient level of dynamism, security, and scrutiny to regular traffic over the borders. One possible answer to this dilemma was given by Dennis Bayle, who states, "the 21st century calls for more openness, not less" (2005). For Bayle, as a U.S. Department of State advisor and specialist in information technology, American society should be more open, while implementing "technologies to engender liberty, such as transparency, secure information, biometrics, surveillance, facial recognition and data mining" (Bayle, 2005). Many of these have already been implemented after 9/11.

Unfortunately for Mexico and the U.S., as Dennis Bayle (2005) points out, transnational organized crime is another factor to consider in the openness dilemma. Since NAFTA's implementation, transnational organized crime has used its channels to move drugs, guns, and money (Arrollo, 2003).

Studies of the border such as those by Laura Carlsen, a specialist in Latin America from the Mexican Center for International Policy, show a complex situation (Carlsen, 2011). The Mexican-U.S. border is one of the biggest shared-land borders of the world. Tijuana, in Baja California, and San Ysidro, in California, is the most crowded entry point of the world. According to the International Monetary Fund (2011), Mexico is the second U.S. commercial partner for the U.S. and the U.S. is the first for Mexico. Since the implementation of NAFTA, more than five million trucks cross the border every year, carrying about the 70 percent of all U.S.–Mexican trade. David and Richard Lebow, from Dartmouth College, cite an estimated cost of U.S. $250 billion in trade, making the Mexican–U.S. border unique and impossible to close, despite the immigration problem (Lebow & Lebow, 2007).

Analysis shows that NAFTA became a haven for transnational organized crime. Tons of marijuana, cocaine, heroin, and methamphetamines ride NAFTA's arteries inside Mexican trucks that cross the border into U.S. metropolitan areas. In return, billions of U.S. dollars and weapons find their way back into Mexico, forcing both governments to develop strategies to control what William Mendell calls "government priorities" against the transnational organized crime threat (Mendel & Munger, 1996).

As Gabriela Moreno's article "Drug Crisis in the Americas" points out, "the U.S. has participated in the war against the illicit drug trade in the Americas, through funding and policymaking" (Moreno, 2009). Based on information presented by the U.S. government, we can say that interdiction at the production site and in-route countries has not given the desired outcomes, creating balloon effects in Latin American countries such as Mexico.

4.   Conclusion

The North America Free-Trade Agreement is a very important strategy for North America. It was developed to enhance economic partnership and create a more prosperous region. However, NAFTA was not a holistic approach in terms of strategic planning (Schwartz, 1996), nor did it follow the "art of the long view" (Mintzber, 1994). NAFTA left the window open for threats such as the transnational organized crime, and terrorism (Bayle, 2005), which on September 11, 2001 demonstrated their ability to attack.

Analyzing the SPP, we can find further security strategies for filling NAFTA's deficiencies with regard to security issues. NAFTA's vacuum in the security field was a contributing factor for the 9/11 attacks to occur, based on the "U.S. society openness paradox" (Bayle, 2005). We can conclude that the attacks were a balloon effect from NAFTA in terms of Bayle's societal openness paradox, which made those places where the attacks took place the weakest link in the U.S. security chain, in terms of their geopolitical location.

IV. MEXICO'S SINGLE-CASE STUDY

A. INTRODUCTION

In the longitudinal analysis developed in Chapter III, we considered three U.S. strategies that precipitated balloon effects in Mexico and determined that, due to geopolitical and economic factors, Mexico suffers a proximity disadvantage in terms of security. We also found that there were balloon-effect counter-pressures against the government that initiated the original action.

In this chapter, we present a single-case study about the Mexican strategy against transnational organized crime to analyze balloon–effect pressures and counter-pressures, following the methodology of George and Bennett (2005).

B. BACKGROUND

The sudden increase in crime and violence in some Mexican cities and regions has raised security concerns not only in Mexico, but also in the U.S. (Brownfield, 2011c; U.S. Department of Justice, National Intelligence Center, 2011). Unfortunately, according to the balloon-effect concept, this undesired behavior cannot be isolated from Mexico's strategy against transnational organized crime. According to Anderson and Johnson, the Mexican strategy was the "point of intervention" unbalancing the "vicious cycle" (Anderson & Johnson, 1997).

The official number of casualties presented by the Mexican government, according the U.S. Congressional Research Service in their August 15, 2011 report, shows that were more than 34,500 casualties related to organized-crime violence from January 2007 to December 2010, without considering an estimated 11,000 casualties estimated in the current year, 2011 (Presidencia de la Republica Mexicana, 2011; United States Government Accountability Office, 2010). These high figures represent secondary balloon effects of the strategy against transnational organized crime.

According to a press conference given by the U.S. assistant secretary of the Bureau of International Narcotics and Law Enforcement Affairs, Williams R.

Brownfield, in Ciudad Juarez on September 2011 (Brownfield, 2011c), this escalated violence has raised American concerns about instability in Mexico and the possibility of violence spilling onto U.S. territory. The U.S. Department of Justice has stated that "the U.S. considers that any political or economic instability in Mexico will impact the U.S. interest" (U.S. Department of Justice, National Intelligence Center, 2011).

C. THE MEXICAN STRATEGY´S POINT OF INTERVENTION

In 2006, newly elected President Calderon determined to confront transnational organized crime as part of his national-security strategy (Presidencia de la Republica Mexicana, 2007b). President Calderón said, "Mexican society could no longer coexist with transnational organized crime." From that point, the Mexican armed forces were sent to confront criminal organizations at the local and regional levels, creating operations such as "Juarez," "Guerrero," "Michoacán," "Tijuana," etc. (Presidencia de la Republica Mexicana, 2007a).

In October 2007, after Calderon´s initial action, the Mexican government requested U.S. government support in the fight, creating the Merida Initiative.

According to the U.S. State Department, "the Merida Initiative is a multiyear program developed among the United States, Mexico, the nations of Central America, the Dominican Republic and Haiti, created to confront the transnational organized crime whose illicit actions undermine public safety, erode the rule of law, and threaten the national security of the United States, considering the furthering respect for human rights and the rule of law, and based on principles of shared responsibility, mutual trust, and respect for sovereign and independence of the signatory states" (U.S. State Department, 2009).

Analyzing the situation for the balloon effect, we can say that the high-impact operations against transnational organized crime were, in the term of Anderson and Johnson, the Mexican "point of intervention" that unbalanced the criminal structure (Anderson & Johnson, 1997). The successes of the Mexican strategy in those places where it was enacted put pressure on the criminal system, forcing perpetrators to migrate elsewhere to continue their activities.

Brownfield also mentioned that the relevance of the Merida Initiative resides in its origins in the "lessons-learned strategy" (2011c) of previous strategies. Using historical examples, the Merida Initiative puts together the pros and the cons of the 1882 Chinese exclusion act, the 1969 operations Intercept and Cooperation, and the 1997 NAFTA and SPP.

D. THE HIGH-IMPACT OPERATION AND MERIDA-INITIATIVE KINSHIP TIES

Following the traditional causality dilemma of the chicken and the egg, U.S. and Mexico are blaming each other about the root of the drug problem: supply or demand?

Since Operation Cooperation's implementation in 1969, the war on drugs has been led by the U.S., following a supply-side approach, and not its internal consumption, while Mexico's approach has been just reactive in terms of trafficking, blaming U.S. for consumption, as implied by balloon effects observed in Mexican homeland security (Ribando, Wyler, & Beittel, 2010). As found in the 2010, U.S. Congressional Research Service Report, the U.S. pledge to Mexico has been to intensify its efforts against transnational criminal organizations, while the Mexican pledge to the U.S. has been to address drug demand and the illicit trafficking of firearms and bulk currency to Mexico (Ribando et al., 2010).

E. THE FIVE PILLARS OF HIGH-IMPACT OPERATIONS

During his presidential campaign, Calderon's pledges were mainly in the social arena. His political platforms were specifically identified as "the government of the job, and poverty, delinquency, and crime reduction." However, it is a tradition in Mexico that after every turnover, the new government performs an impressive action to show its legitimacy, power, and independence from its predecessor.

Accordingly, President Calderon at the beginning of his mandate embraced the fight against transnational organized crime, implementing high-impact operations against this threat to society (Presidencia de la Republica Mexicana, 2007a; Presidencia de la Republica Mexicana, 2007b).

Calderon realized that the deeply outdistance in security matters would endanger a good Mexican lifestyle and national development (Presidencia de la Republica Mexicana, 2011). His government developed National Security Strategy 2007–2012, which consists of five pillars:

- Joint operations to support local authorities and society
- Operational and technological improvement of the federal forces
- Improvements and reforms of the legal system
- Active and efficient law enforcement
- Strengthened national and international cooperation

After implementing high-impact operations, President Calderón started negotiations with the U.S. government, asking to develop an integrated strategy. Ironically, the Mexican government was using the same approach employed by the U.S. in terms of drugs eradication, interdiction, and law enforcement (U.S. State Department, 2009).

According to Alberto Arrollo, the Mexican request was developed under the same approach that the U.S. used, which was to tackle the problem in the production and in-route countries (Arrollo, 2003); or as Assistant Secretary Brownfield noted, Merida is a "lessons-learned" operation (Brownfield, 2011a).

F.   MERIDA INITIATIVE'S FOUR PILLARS

The Merida Initiative may be analyzed from a logistical and operational perspective. According to the U.S., the Merida Initiative´s main areas of interest are improving citizen safety, supporting the fight against transnational organized crime, stopping and avoiding government corruption and the illicit trafficking of arms, people, and money, and building strong and resilient communities able to withstand the pressures of the transnational organized crime, extend U.S. borders of interdiction far away from its territory (U.S. State Department, 2009). As mentioned, all support activities. From the Mexican perspective, the Merida Initiative is a bilateral effort to support stronger democratic institutions, especially the federal forces and judiciary, using formal and civil-society organizations (Secretaría de Gobernación, 2007).

According to the 2011 U.S. Government Accountability Office report:

> The U.S. Congress has appropriated for Mexico $352 million in Fiscal Year 2008, $768 million in 2009, $210.3 million in 2010, and $143 million in 2011 making a total of $ 1,648 million without considering the $281.8 million requested for 2012.

This represents 84 percent of the total amount allocated for Mexico (see Figure 1).

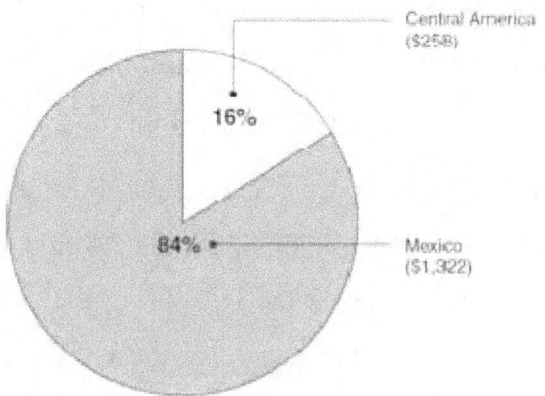

Figure 1.   Total Merida Funds Allocated by Region, Fiscal Year 2008 Through Fiscal Year 2010 (in Millions of Dollars) (From Government Accountability Office 2010)

- ***Break the power and impunity of criminal organizations.*** Merida programs have also been used to assist in the technical development of "Plataforma Mexico" (U.S. Department of Justice, National Intelligence Center, 2011). Plataforma Mexico is one of the largest integrated criminal databases in the world.

  Applying what Brownfield calls lessons learned from previous experiences, Mexico is improving its capacities in the biometric-identification field (Brownfield, 2011a). This was one of Dennis Bayle's recommendations after the 9/11 terrorist attacks, which were attributed by Bayle to the open-society paradox brought on by NAFTA (Bayle, 2005) and which we have considered as a balloon effect.

- ***Assist the Mexican and Central American governments in strengthening border, air, and maritime controls.*** The Mexican federal forces committed to the fight against transnational organized crime have received air assets to increase their air mobility (U.S. Department of Justice, National Intelligence Center, 2011).

- *Curtail gang activity in Mexico and Central America and diminish the demand for drugs in the U.S.* Using local nongovernmental organizations, the Mexican government is improving its educational system, at school and through use of media, by teaching a culture of lawfulness (U.S. Department of Justice, National Intelligence Center, 2011). The goal is to make this education part of Mexico's standard curriculum by the year of 2014 (Presidencia de la Republica Mexicana, 2011).

President Calderon, according to William Brownfield, has shown a commitment to pursuing a common purpose with the U.S., aligning the countries' common interests in the longstanding war on drugs (Brownfield, 2011a).

As a result of these actions, we conclude that President Calderon's government is the link between high-impact operations and the Merida Initiative, creating the first balloon-effect counter-pressure inside the U.S. From the strategy's perspective, we can say that when we talk about achievements, we are talking about high-impact-operation successes, with support from the Merida Initiative at the strategic level.

G.   A COMBINED EFFORT IN A HOLLISTIC APPROACH

According a statement by President Calderon in July 2011, when he came in power, transnational organized crime was challenging local authorities in regions inside Mexico; consequently, the federal government reestablished its authority by sending the armed forces to police the streets (Presidencia de la Republica Mexicana, 2007a). The government used what Graham Turbiville calls "multi-mission force" (Turbiville, 2007), a professional, better-trained and -organized type of force. Calderon said that, through federal forces, the government planned to confront criminal organizations and apply the rule of law.

At the operational level, the Mexican government designated those places with the highest incidence of transnational, organized crime as hot spots, enacting national high-impact operations against them. In one hot spot, Michoacán, the federal government sent 5,000 armed forces to curtail regional violence and crime (Presidencia de la Republica Mexicana, 2007a). Paraphrasing the government's initial statement, the mission of the federal forces was to dismantle cartel organizations by targeting their leaders, causing internal damage to the cartels and further implosion (Presidencia de la Republica Mexicana, 2007a; Presidencia de la Republica Mexicana, 2011).

According to Calderon (2011), from December 2006 to August 2011, federal forces secured 108.9 tons of cocaine, 9,351 tons of marijuana, 3,651 kilograms of opium, 1,798 kilograms of heroin, 57,900 ground vehicles, 431 maritime vessels, 546 aircraft, more than 49,600 small weapons, 70,220 large weapons, 12.7 million rounds of ammunition, and 10,181granades; from just September 2010 to July 2011, 1,185 laboratories for synthetic drugs were dismantled. According to the federal law-enforcement department (PGR)'s most-wanted list, 21 out of 37 cartel leaders have been imprisoned during the last five years; as of August 2011, the Mexican government has extradited 464 criminals to foreign countries (Calderon, 2011). According to a Mexican government report, this is 190 percent more than any other administration (Presidencia de la Republica Mexicana, 2011).

Analyzing the 2007–2012 national-security strategy, we find that its holistic approach includes more than face-to-face confrontations. For instance, it includes the creation of local institutions against kidnapping that support not only the victim, but the family as well. According to President Calderón, since the beginning of the administration, 5,725 victims were freed, 6,560 kidnappers imprisoned, and 902 organizations dismantled (Calderon, 2011).

Based on the national-security strategy, supported by the Merida Initiative, the federal government developed a new network to send and receive intelligence information, the Plataforma Mexico. Using this platform, the federal police have integrated more than four million operations among agencies, improving the operational and technological capability of the federal forces (Presidencia de la Republica Mexicana, 2011).

The armed forces have improved their operational resources by the acquisition of six cougar helicopters; 170 armored vehicles, and 10 small boats. The Mexican navy built mobile headquarters for infantry battalions in regions with a greater criminality index, supported by a new naval-intelligence unit (Presidencia de la Republica Mexicana, 2011).

47

The Mexican government also created a civil-security force of more than 35,000 members equipped with new technology. To professionalize the police force, the government implemented a program to warrant its institutional development and professional stability. During 2011, more than 1,000 college students joined "the new, scientific police branch" (Presidencia de la Republica Mexicana, 2011).

In terms of the human-rights protections, the Mexican strategy added, among other measures, an immigration law seeking to protect against immigration from Central and South America (Presidencia de la Republica Mexicana, 2007b).

One of Mexico's main concerns was the open-society paradox (Bayle, 2005). The government is recovering open spaces such as playgrounds, stadiums, and public spaces, trying to motivate society towards a better way of life (Presidencia de la Republica Mexicana, 2007b). According to the latest presidential address to the nation, 4,050 public spaces have been recovered since 2006 (Presidencia de la Republica Mexicana, 2011).

Using social programs, the Mexican government seeks to reintegrate into society those who abuse drugs or alcohol. At the schools, the program "School Secure" assures that no violence, drugs, or alcohol is introduced at any school. Thirty-six thousand municipal schools have been introduced to this program (Presidencia de la Republica Mexicana, 2011).

H.   MEXICO'S INTERNATIONAL COOPERATION

The Mexican government is strengthening links with the international community. As the recipient of previous balloon effects, the Mexican government understands that unilateral effort against a common threat does not work. Consequently, Mexico has used international forums such as the United Nations and the Organization of American States to develop further agreements (Brownfield, 2011a; Presidencia de la Republica Mexicana, 2011). This was the framework President Calderon used in 2007 to ask for U.S. assistance to develop Merida Initiative strategy.

I. MERIDA'S INVESTMENTS

According to the 2010 U.S. Government Accountability Office report, the Merida Initiative's initial estimated cost was $1.6 billion USD (United States Government Accountability Office, 2010). By the end of this year, as confirmed by William Brownfield in a press conference in Washington D.C., the U.S. government will have delivered more than $900 million worth of support to Mexico (Brownfield, 2011a). Considering the Merida Initiative as a support strategy from the Mexican perspective, we can consider the money given by the U.S. to support high-impact operations as an investment in the security field.

According to President Calderon, the Mexican government invested during the Merida initial stage approximately $26 billion USD out of its own resources (Calderon, 2011). This represents a rough relationship of 17.3:1; that is, for every U.S. dollar invested in the Merida Initiative, Mexico has invested 17.3.

In testimony in Washington D.C. on October 4, 2011, Assistant Secretary Brownfield succinctly mentioned that the Merida Initiative is not a "strategy" [program] against the Mexican drug cartels or criminal actors, nor was its vision a panacea for the illicit activities fueling the violence inside Mexico (Brownfield, 2011b). Mr. Brownfield also mentioned that the Merida Initiative was created "to strengthen Mexico's institutional capacity to counter crime and enforce the rule of law (Brownfield, 2011a).

J. HIGH-IMPACT OPERATIONS ACHIEVEMENTS USING MERIDA-INITIATIVE SUPPORT

According to the July 2010 Government Accountability Office report (United States Government Accountability Office, 2010), the U.S. has delivered equipment and training under the Merida Initiative, which represents 46 percent of the total amount obligated for:

- Aircraft and boats to support interdiction activities and rapid response of law enforcement entities and other security forces.

- Inspection equipment and canine units to facilitate interdiction of trafficked drugs, arms, cash, explosives, and persons.

- Technical advice and training to strengthen the institutions of justice and law enforcement.

- Crime-prevention programs that address the root causes of crime and violence, specifically among youth.

Following the information provided by both governments, we found that the most recent and important achievements are linked to high-impact operations and the Merida Initiative's four pillars.

1.   Disrupt Organized Criminal Groups

The Mexican federal forces received pilot and maintenance training and air assets to increase their air mobility (see Table 1). Using some of these aircraft, Mexico has removed or arrested 33 high-value targets, including four of the top seven most-wanted criminals designated by the Mexican government. Reciprocally, Mexico has extradited some of the main cartel leaders to U.S. in an expeditious manner.

In December 2010, the Mexican federal police conducted a successful operation, against the Familia cartel (cartel La Familia Michoacána), which inflicted severe damage to the organization, targeting one of its founders, and detaining other members.

In September 2011, using Black Hawk helicopters provided under Merida, the Mexican navy carried out a raid on a Zetas cartel training base in Nuevo Leon (Direccion de Comunicacion Social SEMAR, 2011b), arresting 19 cartel members and seizing guns, money, and communication systems (Direccion de Comunicacion Social SEMAR, 2011a).

Table 1.   Selected Equipment and Training Delivered to Mexico and Central America
Under the Merida Initiative, as of March 21, 2010 (From Government
Accountability Office, 2010)

Table 1: Selected Equipment and Training Delivered to Mexico and Central America under the Mérida Initiative, as of March 31, 2010

	Delivery date*
Mexico	
Equipment	
26 armored vehicles	May 2009
62 Plataforma Mexico computer servers	June 2009
Training equipment	July & December 2009
5 X-ray vans	August 2009
OASISS servers and software	August 2009
Biometric equipment	September 2009 & January 2010
Document verification software	September 2009
Ballistic tracing equipment (IBIS)	September 2009
30 ion scanners	October 2009
Rescue communication equipment & training	October & November 2009
Personal protective equipment	October & November 2009
5 Bell helicopters	December 2009
10 Mobile X-ray minivans	December 2009
Constanza software	February 2010
100 Polygraph units	March 2010
13 armored Suburbans	April 2010
Training	
230 Officials attending arms trafficking conferences	April 2009 to October 2009
187 Mexican Ministry of Public Safety (SSP) officers trained in corrections instruction and classification	April 2009 to December 2009
United Nation's human rights project inaugurated	July 2009
4,392 SSP investigators trained	July 2009 to January 2010
USAID training for capacity building programs throughout Mexico for over 10,000 Mexican officials in the following areas: • Citizen participation councils • Victim protection and restitution • Judicial exchanges • Trafficking in persons • Human rights • Pre-trial services and case resolution alternatives • Continuing education for police, prosecutors and other officials • Penal reform	August 2009 to March 2010
Over 200 Mexican prosecutors and investigators trained in trial advocacy, trafficking in persons, and extradition	September 2009 to March 2010
28 canine trainers trained	October 2009 to April 2010
293 mid-level and senior-level SSP officers trained	October 2009 to November 2009
45 Mexican state officials trained in anti-kidnapping	November 2009 to January 2010

Merida programs have been used to assist in the technical development of Plataforma Mexico, one of the largest integrated criminal databases in the world. Assistance has also helped to develop a biometric identification system, which was used to identify, from the fingerprints database, some of the participants on the August 26, 2011, bombing at the Casino Royale in Monterrey, Nuevo Leon. The case resulted in several Zeta cartel-member detentions.

2. **Strengthen Institutions and Respect for Human Rights**

Under the Merida Initiative, the State Department is working with the state corrections-training academies in Colorado and New Mexico and with the U.S. Federal Bureau of Prisons (Brownfield, 2011b) to provide training and technical assistance for corrections staff in Mexico. This U.S. program is designed as a part of a holistic Mexican program that includes the construction of eighteen federal correction facilities by the end of 2012 (Presidencia de la Republica Mexicana, 2011). According to President Calderon's 2011 address to the nation, and confirmed by Brownfield, resources from the Merida initiative in day-by-day Mexico are building a stronger adherence to the rule of law, respect for human rights, strong institutions, promotion of full civil-society participation, and reformation of the judicial system (Brownfield, 2011b; Presidencia de la Republica Mexicana, 2011).

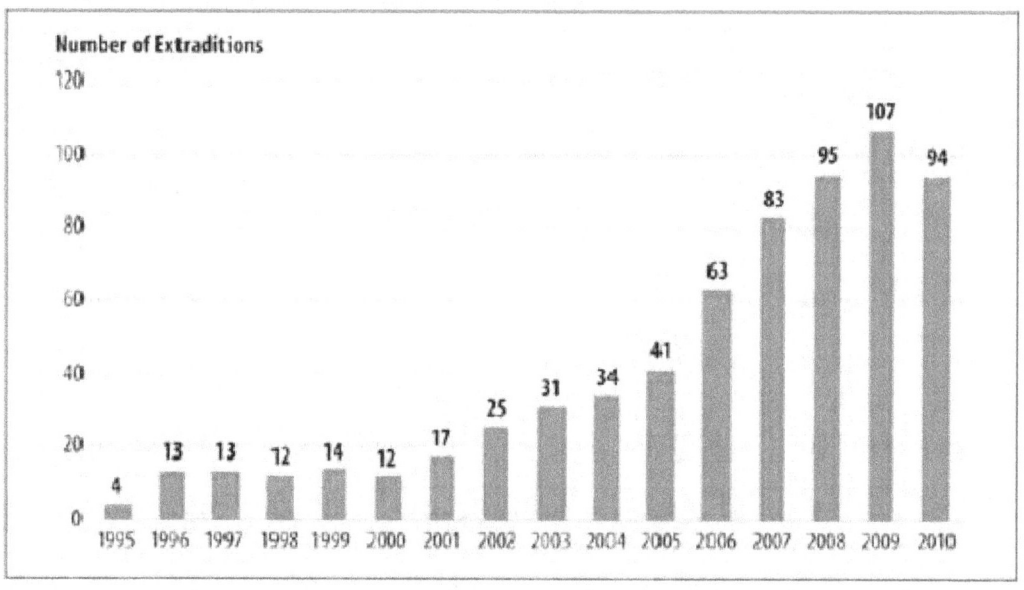

Figure 2. Individuals Extradited from Mexico to United States 1995–2010
(From U.S. Embassy of Mexico [1995–2006 data])

3. **Build a Twenty-First Century Border**

According to the Government Accountability Office report of June 2010, the Merida Initiative has provided new technology devices such as scanners, X-ray machines,

52

and other nonintrusive inspection equipment, similar to those described by Dennis Bayle in *The Open Society Paradox* (2005), to enhance Mexican border officials' ability to detect illicit materials going through entry points (see Table 1).

Special emphasis has been put on supporting law-enforcement operations via specially trained canine teams. The mobility and flexibility of this asset has increased overall seizures of illegal substances, drugs, cash, weapons, people, and other illegal materials traversing the border (Presidencia de la Republica Mexicana, 2011).

According to Calderon, since 2006, 108,900 kilograms of cocaine, 9,351 tons of marijuana, 3,651 kilograms of opium, and 798 kilograms of heroin has been confiscated by federal forces (Calderon, 2011).

4.   Build Strong and Resilient Communities

The Merida Initiative is also helping to build stronger communities in Mexico that can better resist the influence of the cartels by teaching principles of community growth and prosperity based in the common good (Brownfield, 2011b).

K.   BALLOON EFFECTS AND MEASURES OF EFFECTIVENES/ PERFORMANCE

As seen, every time a country develops a strategy, whether unilaterally or in conjunction with another, there are balloon effects in other places. To prove this hypothesis, we have to analyze Mexican high-impact operations against transnational organized crime as a unilateral strategy. We shall test whether this strategy has created balloon effects, where those effects were reflected, and whether it has caused counter-pressures.

As stated by the Mexican government in February 2007, one of the operational objectives of high-impact operations was to damage the cartels through high-target decapitation (Presidencia de la Republica Mexicana, 2007a). This action, according to Anderson and Johnson, is the point of intervention (1997) that unbalances criminal organizational structure, creating a leadership void.

Another situation that fueled violence was the government's success in recovering total control over some regions, forcing the criminals to move to a different place, which created confrontations in places such as Ciudad Juarez and Nuevo Laredo. This is a clear balloon effect: pressure on the cartels forced them to migrate; at their new destination, they fought against themselves, creating the violence on the streets. This is a positive measure of effectiveness, according to the balloon effect, because the strategy applied pressure and forced migration.

In an instance of the balloon effect in the border region, we note that since cartel actives in Tijuana have been diminished by a military presence on the streets, criminal activity has migrated to Ciudad Juarez, and Nuevo Laredo, where these way stations on the NAFTA routes have —fueled by the openness paradox—been used by criminal organizations to move illegal goods.

By the same logic, we can say that another balloon effect of high-impact operations is the migration of criminal activities to new places. These places are now the weakest link in the Mexican security chain, due to their geopolitical locations.

Analyzing the situation under this scope, it is clear that the fight was not created by the Mexican government per se, yet it is a balloon effect of the holistic approach against the organized crime at the macro, meso, and micro level of implementation.

The Mexican and American people may wonder about the strategy′s measures of effectiveness and the armed forces′ measures of performance; some, like Jorge Carrasco, just ignore government successes (Carrasco, 2011), and still others, such as Reyes Garcés (2009), do not see a well-developed strategy and believe the approach should be changed. However, it would be hard to implement different parameters if both countries keep targeting the problem from a different approach. According to the 2010 Congressional Report, *Latin American and the Caribbean; Illicit Drug Trafficking and U.S. Counter Drugs Programs*, long-term goals for both countries may be similar, but the short-term and priorities are different (Ribando et al., 2010). Hence, both countries' focal points will switch to its main area of interest. In Mexico, the may aim be stopping violence, while the U.S. may aim at seizing drugs at entry points.

Even when high-impact operations and the Merida Initiative are tied together, neither losses nor successes can be mixed. From the U.S. perspective, the Merida Initiative is played at the strategic level: training, technical and material support, and costs in terms of money. From the Mexican perspective, the strategy is being played at the operational and tactical level, and costs lives.

L.   STRATEGY´S CONSTRAINTS

As seen in Chapter III, Mexico and the U.S. started their cooperation against transnational organized crime in the late 1960s, with Operation Cooperation. This operation was interrupted because of U.S. mistrust of Mexican officials and government corruption (Ribando et al., 2010). From the Mexican side perspective, the contributive factor, according to Ivelaw Griffith, the certification process and its implications for sovereignty issues from the past (Griffith, 1997).

One of the main constraints against any security cooperation between the countries is the fierce opposition of the Mexican government towards any presence of U.S. officials in active rather than diplomatic positions, based on deep concern about past American intervention in Mexico.

One clear example about this situation is the comment made by Texas Governor Rick Perry. Perry suggested, "It may require our military in Mexico working in concert with them to kill these drug cartels and to keep them off of our border." As mentioned by Catherine E. Shoichet and Rey Rodriguez from CNN, this announcement "riled officials and spurred debate from analysts on both sides of the border" (Shoichet & Rodriguez, 2011). Two days after Perry´s unfortunate statement, the American ambassador to Mexico, Arturo Sarukan (2011), stated, "The matter of the participation or presence of U.S. troops on Mexican soil is not on the table." Sarukan added, "It is not a component that forms part of the innovative approaches that Mexico and the United States have been using to confront transnational organized crime" (2011). In other words: no U.S. boots on Mexican ground. Catherine E. Shoichet and Rey Rodriguez concluded that analysts agree that "the controversial idea could have significant political consequences and security implications—even as a political campaign proposal" (2011).

From the international perspective, the Merida Initiative is a holistic effort made by the governments of Mexico, America, Central America, the Dominican Republic, and Haiti to engage on every front in the battle against transnational organized crime (Gobernación, 2007). From the U.S.–Mexican perspective, Merida's support is a bilateral top-down strategy designed to work in three stages, at the national, state, and local level Gobernación, 2007). As the ambassador to Mexico stated "it´s not a quick-fix: it is an ambitious, multiyear effort to address longstanding problems" (Brownfield, 2011a) or, as Peter Schwartz called it is a matter of "the art of the long view (Schwartz, 1996).

M.   THE MERIDA INITIATIVE TODAY

According to both Mexico and the U.S., the Merida Initiative is in transition. In its first stage, Merida concentrated on delivering equipment and goods and building stronger federal institutions in Mexico. This is shifting towards specialized training, focused at the state and local level (United States Government Accountability Office, 2010). According to William Brownfield in a press conference in Washington D.C. on October 2011, both governments will now support specific areas where Mexico and the U.S. have shared security interests, such as, "the border and drug-trafficking routes where the violence is greatest, due to the negative-influence secondary-order effects of the Merida Initiative" (2011b)—or, as we call them, balloon effects.

N.   BEYOND MERIDA: THE SECOND STAGE

During his most recent visit to Ciudad Juarez, Mexico, Brownfield explained that both countries agree on how to divide Merida in packages of wealth distribution (Brownfield, 2011b). Officials from the Mexico and U.S. have worked jointly to develop new objectives for the initiative, known as "Beyond Merida" (Secretaría de Gobernación, 2007; United States Government Accountability Office, 2010). This second stage is divided into four new pillars, superseding the initial 2008 pillars.

1.   Disrupt Organized Criminal Groups

Increase coordination and information sharing, focusing on intelligence collection and analysis, training and equipping special units, enhancing local police and prosecutorial investigative capacity, conducting targeted investigations against money laundering, improving interdiction, and supporting effective command-and-control centers across Mexico.

2. Institutionalize Reforms to Sustain Rule of Law and Respect for Human Rights

Keep building security and justice institutions at the federal level, expanding these efforts to additional federal, state, and local institutions.

3. Create a Twenty-First Century Border

Maintain citizen safety while increasing global competitiveness thorough efficient and secure flows of two-way commerce and travel on the border.

4. Build Strong and Resilient Communities

Develop programs that will leverage support for local community involvement, develop a culture of lawfulness, and address socioeconomic challenges.

According to a U.S. Congress report in 2010, by the end of 2011, the U.S. will have invested more than $900 million in equipment and training for Mexico (Ribando et al., 2010). As previously mentioned, it is hard to differentiate the source of resources committed to high-impact operations at the macro level of analysis, because it is a Mexican strategy, supported by the Merida Initiative.

O. CONCLUSION

A quote from William Brownfield summarizes what the whole strategy is all about:

> The Merida Initiative was not engraved in stone. It is a living strategy that is modified, adjusted, and corrected as circumstances change on the ground and we learn lessons. Some of those lessons came from the United States Congress. (Brownfield, 2011a)

> It is a valuable idea to integrate our efforts against illicit drugs, organized crime, and terrorism into a unified, holistic approach to support the Merida Initiative. (Brownfield, 2011b)

Brownfield's statements, in terms of the balloon effect and its counter-pressure, allow us to establish two conclusions:

1. The entire strategy is successful, as mentioned by both governments with regard to achievements in the fight against the transnational organized crime (Presidencia de la Republica Mexicana, 2011; U.S. Department of Justice, National Intelligence Center, 2011).

2. Mexico is no longer the weakest link in the Americas security chain, but rather, Latin America is. This claim is made by Ezra Fieser in his studies about the implication of the Mexican strategy on Latin America, Central, South, America, and the Caribbean (Correspondent, 2010; Fieser, 2010; Fieser, 2011). Fieser also cites the resurgence of the Mexican drug cartels in Guatemala, Argentina, and Dominican Republic.

Brownfield summarizes the history of the Merida Initiative by saying it has been positive within Mexican society, due to having been designed as a concerted agreement among countries of the region acting in a preemptive manner. This approach, according to Brownfield, "is another lesson learned from previous strategies, because if those countries were not included in the package they would be latter impacted by negative secondary [balloon] effects" (2011a).

Putting the information within our context, we say that Merida Initiative support was accepted with consideration of factors such as globalization, the open-society paradox, and what Charles Laffiteau calls "problems of unilateralism" in developing a strategy (Laffiteau, 2011).

Giving a Mexican perspective, President Calderon said, "through the 2007–2012 Mexican national-security strategy, the government has strengthened national institutions, taking care of its citizens and local governments while confronting criminal organizations and violence" (Presidencia de la Republica Mexicana, 2011).

V.   CONCLUSION

To be the weakest link in the Americas' security chain means to receive the brunt of second-order effects, or balloon effects, from the strategies of other countries. We have argued that, historically, this has befallen Mexico as the weakest link in Pan-American security and have shown the effects and counter-effects of several unilateral strategies that corroborate our hypothesis.

As seen in this thesis, Mexico and the United States share much more than a border. Together, they are part of what Ulieru calls an "interdependent security ecosystem" (2008). We confirmed that both countries share the threats and challenges of the 21st century, which need to be addressed from a bilateral approach that considers the interaction and capacities of the different and complex organizations involved—not only from the armed forces and federal police to the local police but also the society, at their different locations in both sides of the border.

Mexico's geopolitical fate as the weakest link in the Pan-American security chain has been altered, since 2006, by new Mexican interventions and U.S. government support. As noted by Brownfield, "It is not a quick-fix strategy: it is an ambitious, multiyear effort to address longstanding problems" (2011a). Standing as we are now in the middle of the fight, both countries are experiencing short term and balloon effects, yet there is every hopeful indication for a combined Mexican–American victory in the long term.

THIS PAGE INTENTIONALLY LEFT BLANK

LIST OF REFERENCES

Anderson, V. & Johnson, L. (1997). *System thinking basic: From concepts to causal loops.* Waltham, MA: Pegasus Communications.

Arrollo, A. (2003). *Impacts of the North America free trade agreement in Mexico.* Managua Nicaragua: Ediciones Educativas, Diseño e Impresiones S.A.

Bayle, D. (2005). *The open society paradox.* Dulles, VA: Potomac Books Inc.

Brownfield, W. R. (2011a, October 4). *Is Merida antiquated? Updating U.S. policy to counter threats of insurgency and narco-terror.* Paper presented at the Washington D.C. press conference. Retrieved Septembert 22, 2011, from http://www.state.gov/p/inl/rls/rm/175007.htm

Brownfield, W. R. (2011b, October 4). *Merida part II: Insurgency and terrorism in Mexico.* Paper presented at the Washington D.C. press conference Retrieved September 22, 2011, from http://www.state.gov/p/inl/rls/rm/174982.htm

Brownfield, W. R. (2011c, August 17). *Press conference at the Consulate General, Ciudad Juarez.* Retrieved September 22, 2011, from http://www.state.gov/p/inl/rls/rm/170624.htm

Buchenau, J. (2001, spring). Small numbers, great impact: Mexico and its immigrants, 1821–1973. *Journal of American Ethnic History, 20*(3), 23–50. Retrieved January 12, 2011, from http://www.u.arizona.edu/~rgolden/MexicoImmigration.pdf

Campos, R. (2010). *Percepción Ciudadana Sobre la Seguridad en México.* Retrieved September 10, 2010, from http://www.consulta.mx/Estudio.aspx?Estudio=seguridad-mexico-mucd

Campos, R. (2011). *Felipe Calderón-Evaluación 19 Trimestre de Gobierno.* Retrieved February 11,, 2011, from http://www.consulta.mx/Estudio.aspx?Estudio=evagob-na

Carlsen, L., & Fefeer, J. (2007, February 12). NAFTA kicked up at notch. *Foreign Policy in Focus.* Retrieved from http://www.fpif.org/articles/nafta_kicked_up_a_notch

Carlsen, L. (2011, February 15). *NAFTA's security agenda. Americas Program.* Retrieved March 01, 2011, from http://www.cipamericas.org/archives/1583

Carrasco Araizaga, J. (2011). Victoria inalcanzable. *Proceso,* 6–10.

Chinese Exclusion Act, 22 Stat. 58 (1882).

Clare Ribando, S., Wyler, J. S., & Beittel, J. S. (2010). *Latin America and the Caribbean; illicit drug trafficking and U.S. counter drug programs* (No. 41215). Washington DC: Congressional Reseach Service.

Correspondent, E. F. (2010, November 5). Drug wars in Mexico, Colombia push drug trade to Dominican Republic; as authorities in Mexico and Colombia crack down on the drug trades in their countries and the US-Mexico border becomes harder to sneak across, drug rings are moving their operations into the Caribbean. *The Christian Science Monitor*.

Craig, R. (1991). Operacion Intercepcion: Una Política de Presión Internacional. *Foro Internacional, 22*(2), 203–230. Retrieved December 3, 2011, from http://www.jstor.org/stable/27737335

Craig, R. B. (1980). Operation intercept: The international politics of pressure. *The Review of Politics, 42*(4), 556–580.

Crandall, R., Paz, G., & Roett, R. (2005). In Crandall R., Paz G.& Roett R. (Eds.), *Mexico's democracy at work*. Boulder, CO: Lynner Rienner Publishers.

Cummings, J. (2001). *Mexicali's Chinatown: Sharks fin tacos and barbecued chow mein.* Retrieved July 3, 2011, from http://www.cpamedia.com/history/sharks_fin_tacos/

Curtis, J. R. (1995). Mexicali Chinatown. *Geographical Review, 85*(3), 335–348. Retrieved March 5, 2011, from http://www.little-yeti.com/idh3931-co/readings/02-28/Mexicali%27s%20Chinatown.pdf

Deitch, R. (2003). *HEMP-American history revisited: A plant with a divided history* (3rd ed.). New York: Algora Publishing.

Direccion de Comunicacion Social SEMAR. (2011a). *Asegura la Armada a 19 Presuntos Integrantes del Grupo Delictivo de los Zetas en un Campo de Entrenamiento en Nuevo León.* Retrieved September 22, 2011, from http://www.semar.gob.mx/sitio_2/sala-prensa/comunicados-2011/1904-comunicado-de-prensa-293-2011.html

Direccion de Comunicacion Social SEMAR. (2011b). *Recibe la Secretaria de Marina-Armada de Mexico Nuevos Helicopteros Black Hawk.* Retrieved September 22, 2011, from http://www.semar.gob.mx/sitio_2/sala-prensa/comunicados-2011/1899-comunicado-de-prensa-288-2011.html

Doyle, K. (2011). *Operation Intercept the perils of unilateralism.* Retrieved August 13, 2011, from http://www.gwu.edu/~nsarchiv/NSAEBB/NSAEBB86/

Epple, D. & Platt, G. J. (1998). Equilibrium and local redistribution in an urban economy when households differ in both preferences and incomes. *Journal of Urban Economics*, *43*(1), 23–51. Retrieved November 22, 2011, from http://www.sciencedirect.com/science/article/pii/S0094119096920306

Fieser, E. (2010). Drug wars in Mexico, Colombia push drug trade to Dominican republic. *The Christian Science Monitor*, 1–2.

Fieser, E. (2011, June). Guatemala invasion of Mexico's drug cartels. *Tucson Sentinel*, 15-30. Retrieved September 25, 2011, from http://www.tucsonsentinel.com/nationworld/report/061311_guatemala_gangs/guatemala-invasion-mexicos-drug-cartels/

Foot, R., MacFarlane, S. N., & Mastanduno, M. (2003). In Foot R., MacFarlane S. N. and Mastanduno M. (Eds.), *US hegemony and international organizations: The United States and multilateral institutions*. New York: Oxford University Press.

Fowler, T. B. (1996). The international narcotics trade: Can it be stopped by interdiction? *Journal of Policy Modeling*, *18*(3), 233–270. doi: 10.1016/0161-8938(95)00071-2

George, A. L. & Bennett, A. (2005). *Case studies and theory development in the social science*. Cambridge Massachusetts: Center for Science and International Affairs John F, Kennedy School of Government Harvard University.

Gooberman, L. A. (1974). Operation Intercept: The multiple consequences of a public policy. *Drug Information Articles*. Retrieved September 25, 2011, from http://www.druglibrary.org/schaffer/history/e1960/intercept/default.htm

Griffith, I. L. (1997). *Drugs and security in the Caribbean: Sovereignty under siege*. Pennsylvania: Pennsylvania State University Press.

Interdepartmental Task Force. (1969). Report of special task force relating to narcotics, marihuana and dangerous drugs. Retrieved September 26, 2011, http://www.druglibrary.org/schaffer/history/e1960/intercept/members.htm

International Monetary Fund. (2011). *World economic groups*. Washington DC: author. Retrieved October 22, 2011, from http://www.imf.org/external/pubs/ft/weo/2011/01/weodata/weoselgr.aspx

Kenneth, M. (2010). Mexico and the cocaine epidemic: The new Colombia or a new problem? Master's thesis, Naval Postgraduate School, Monterey, CA.

Laffiteau, C. (2011). The balloon effect: The failure of supply side strategies in the war on drugs. *Academia.Edu*, *1*, 1–18. Retrieved November 20, 2011, from http://www.academia.edu/

Lawrence A, G. (1974). *Operation intercept: The multiple consequences of a public policy*. New York: Pergamon Press INC.

Lebow, D., & Lebow, R. N. (2007). *Unilateralism across the border: U.S.–Mexican relations and the war on terror*. Retrieved August 14, 2011, from http://www.dartmouth.edu/~nedlebow/mexico.pdf

Malone, D. M., & Khong, Y. F. (2001). *Unilateralism and U.S. foreign policy; international perspectives*. United States of America: Lynne Rienner Publishers, Inc.

Meiners, S. (2009). Central America; an emerging role in the drug trade. *Central America*.

Mendel, W. W., & Munger, M. D. (1996). The drug threat; getting priorities straight.*27* (2), 110–124.

The Merida Initiative. (2009). Retrieved July 2, 2011, from http://www.state.gov/p/inl/rls/fs/122397.htm

Mexicans launched operation dignity. (1969, October 2 1969). *The Modesto Bee,* pp. B4. Retrieved January 19, 2011, from http://news.google.com/newspapers?nid=1948&dat=19691002&id=z8RJAAAAI BAJ&sjid=Bx0NAAAAIBAJ&pg=1178,380718

Mintzber, H. (1994). *The rise and fall of strategic planning; Reconceiving roles for planning, plans, planners*. New York: Simon & Schuster Inc.

Mintzber, H., Ahlstrand, B., & Lampel, J. (1998). *Strategy safari; A guided tour through the wilds of strategic management*. New York: Simon & Schuster Inc.

Moreno, G. (2009). *The drug crisis in the Americas*. Houston, TX: Center for International Studies, University St. Thomas.

Napolitano, J., & Department of Homeland Security. (2009). Administration officials announce U.S.-Mexico border security policy: A comprehensive response & commitment. Washington, DC: White House.

Nixon, R. (July, 1969). *Special message to the congress on control of narcotics and dangerous drugs.* Retrieved September 3, 2011, from http://www.presidency.ucsb.edu/ws/?pid=2126

Nye Jr., J. S. (2004). *Bound to lead: The changing nature of American power* (2nd ed.). New York: Public Affairs.

Pardo, G. (2008). *La Migración China a América es Incontrolable.* Retrieved May 17, 2011, from http://www.voltairenet.org/La-migracion-china-a-America-es

Payan, T. (2006). *The three U.S.-Mexico border wars; Drugs, immigration, and homeland security.* Westport, CT, London: Praeger Security International.

Presidencia de la Republica Mexicana. (2007a). *Anuncio sobre la Operación Conjunta Michoacán.* Retrieved November 11, 2010, from http://www.presidencia.gob.mx/2006/12/anuncio-sobre-la-operacion-conjunta-michoacan/

Plan Nacional de Desarrollo. (2007b). Retrieved July 9, 2011, from http://pnd.calderon.presidencia.gob.mx/eje1.html

Presidencia de la Republica Mexicana. (2011). *5to. Informe de Gobierno.* Mexico DF: Mexico DF? Retrieved Novembert 5, 2011, from http://quinto.informe.gob.mx/

Reyes Garces, A. (2009). *Winning the war on drugs in Mexico? Toward and integrated approach to the Illegal drug trade.* Master's thesis, Naval Postgraduate School, Monterey, CA.

Reyes Tépach, M. (2006). *Indicadores Delictivos por Estados y el Presupuesto Público Federal que la Federación Asigna a las Entidades Federativas para la Seguridad Pública 1999-2006* No. SE-ISS-05-06). Mexico DF: Centro de Documentación Información y Análisis. Retrieved October 3, 2011, from http://www.diputados.gob.mx/cedia/sia/se/SE-ISS-05-06.pdf

Ribando Seelke, C. & M. Finklea, K. (2011). *U.S.-Mexico security cooperation: The Merida initiative and beyond* (Report for Congress No. 41349). Washington DC: United States Government. Retrieved July 23, 2011, from http://www.fas.org/sgp/crs/row/R41349.pdf; www.crs.gov

Rollins, J., Wyler, L. S., & Rosen, S. (2010). *International terrorism and transnational crime: Security threats, U.S. policy, and considerations for congress* (Report for Congress No. R41004). Retrieved from http://fpc.state.gov/documents/organization/134960.pdf

Schwartz, P. (1996). *The art of the long view; Planning for the future in an uncertain world.* New York: Double Day.

Secretaría de Gobernación. (2007). *Iniciativa Mérida.* Retrieved May 15, 2011, from http://www.iniciativamerida.gob.mx/

Schiavone Camacho, J. M. (2009). Crossing boundaries, claiming a homeland: The Mexican-Chinese transpacific journey to becoming Mexican, 1910s–1960s. *Pacific Historical Review, 78*(4), 547–565. Retrieved April 8, 2011, from http://lasa.international.pitt.edu/members/congress-papers/lasa2009/files/SchiavoneCamachoJuliaMaria.pdf

Shoichet, C. E., & Rodriguez, R. (2011). *Perry's suggestion to send U.S. troops south riles Mexican officials*. Retrieved September 4, 2011, from http://www.cnn.com/2011/10/03/politics/mexico-us-troops/index.html

Smith, P. H. (2008). *Talons of the eagle Latin America, the United States, and the world* (3rd ed.). New York: Oxford University Press.

Teichman, J. E. (2001). *The politics of freeing markets in Latin America: Chile, Argentina, and Mexico*. Chapel Hill, NC: University of North Carolina Press.

Televisa (Producer), & Clio (Director). (2002). *Chiapas la Guerra y la Paz*. [Video/DVD] Mexico D.F.: Video Máximo S.A. de C.V.

Toro, Maria Celia (1992). *Are American control drug policies exacerbating or addressing the country's drug problems?* XVII Congress of the Latin American Studies Association .Los Angeles CA. Retrieved August 3, 2011, from http://lasa.international.pitt.edu/members/congress-papers/lasa1992/files/ToroMariaCelia.pdf

Turbiville Jr., G. H. (2007). Law enforcement and the Mexican armed forces: A new internal security missions challenge the military. *Foreign Military Studies Office, Military Review*. Retrieved July 28, 2011, from http://fmso.leavenworth.army.mil/documents/mxcoparm.htm

U.S. Department of Justice, National Intelligence Center. (2011). *National drug threat assessment 2011* (No. 2011-Q0317-001).

U.S. Department of State (2005).*Security and prosperity partnership of North America: An overview and selected issues*. Retrieved July 30, 2011, from http://fpc.state.gov/c18185.htm

Ulieru, M. (2008). A complex systems approach to the design and evaluation of security ecosystems. *Canada Research Chair*. Retrieved October 15, 2011, from http://www.cs.unb.ca/~ulieru/Publications/Boston-submitted.pdf

United States Government Accountability Office. (2010). *Merida initiative: The United States has provided counter narcotics and anticrime support but needs better performance measures* (Report to Congressional Requesters No. 10-837). Washington DC: United States Government. Retrieved May 19, 2011, from http://www.state.gov/p/inl/rls/rm/175007.htm

Whitworth, S. S. (2008). *The untold story of Mexico's rise and eventual monopoly of the methamphetamine trade*. Master's thesis, Naval Postgraduate School, Monterey, CA.